DO NOT DISTURB

*How two council estate kids
went on to buy their own hotel.*

Neil Kirby

Do Not Disturb

Published by Neil Kirby

Copyright © Neil Kirby 2024

The right of Neil Kirby to be identified as the author of this work has been asserted by them in accordance with the Copyright, Designs and Patents Act 1988.

All rights reserved. No part of this publication may be reproduced, transmitted, or stored in a retrieval system, in any form or by any means, without permission in writing from the publisher, nor be otherwise circulated in any form of binding or cover other than that in which it is published and without a similar condition being imposed on the subsequent purchaser.

Book contents formatted by:
James Harvey – soulsong.co.uk

ISBN: 9-798-341-174-313

This book is dedicated to my darling wife, Wendy, our children, Nicola, Neil Junior and David. Grandchildren, Katie, Ben, George, Joseph, Elizabeth, Olivia and Annabelle.

Do Not Disturb

Acknowledgements:

I have spent five decades in the Hotel Industry loved every minute of it, working with some great people who have ensured we looked after our customers with special personal service, delivered time after time ensuring that the customer is always king. Appetising food, cleanliness, not only in all bedrooms, but also all public areas, attention to detail and, most importantly, a family run hotel.

Thank you to Simon Brown my General Manager and with me for over 27 years, Michael Titherington our Executive Head Chef and Deputy Manager, his wife Claire Titherington on reception, and all my Team here at the Langham Hotel. Thank you also to all my wonderful customers.

A final thanks to Bob Harris for his help, advice and patience in helping me produce this book, not an easy task after the success of my first book, CELEBRITY HOTEL.

Neil Kirby

September 2024

Introduction

Having spent much of my life either travelling, staying in hotels or writing, it was a no brainer when Neil Kirby, owner of top Eastbourne hostelry, the Langham Hotel, asked me if I would cast an eye over his manuscript for the second part of his autobiography, this one entitled, *Do Not Disturb*.

It happened almost by chance as I took my friend David Bedford, the former 10,000 metres world record holder and London Marathon race director, to join compulsive long distance runner Neil and his equally infatuated son Neil Jnr, for lunch in their elegantly refurbished hotel. The idea was for Dave to spend a couple of days back in the seaside resort he visited so often to stay with his grandfather during school holidays and be the celebrity starter for the annual marathons organised by the younger of the two Neils. These races took in the glorious South Downs, my new hometown of Eastbourne and the world-renowned Beachy Head.

While "Bootsie" – you remember him for his trademark droopy moustache and red socks – was only too delighted to help, Neil senior told me about his idea of following up his enormously successful first book *Celebrity Hotel* and tentatively enquired if I would help with a second.

While most of my life was spent journeying around the globe covering major sports events for a variety of newspapers, I have also enjoyed writing books and penned a couple of dozen, several with the late and much-missed Sir Bobby Robson, cricketers Sir Viv Richards, Sir Garfield Sobers and Dennis Lillee, as well as a plethora of footballers including a couple of all-time greats, John Charles and Denis Law, plus serious characters, Bruce Grobbelaar, Graeme Souness, Steve Coppell, Stuart Pearce, Kevin Keegan, Terry Butcher and Graham Kelly. Add to that a Holocaust survivor's tale in *The Boxer's Story*, and you get a fair idea of what I have been doing with my life.

Do Not Disturb

I had a few horror stories to tell as well, such as the 1972 Munich Olympic Games massacre; The Heysel Stadium disaster in Brussels and the catastrophe of the Hillsborough semi-final, events when the joys of sport turn to a shock that lasts a lifetime, and there was no counselling in those days! You simply got on with the next assignment.

Neil is a kindred spirit, in that he loves sport, particularly running, a sport in which he has raised hundreds of thousands of pounds for a variety of charities with his efforts, including a world record at the age of seventy! But more of that later in his book.

It was the hotel side which really enticed me. Despite having spent so many nights in so many hotel rooms, in so many countries, it was a subject I have never really explored, and it fascinated me no end. Expenses generously provided by my newspaper employers ensured that most of the time I was coddled and well looked after, usually in four-star or five-star hotels, with only the odd traumatic exception. But it was what went on behind the front of house which really captured my imagination, as Neil took down the *Do Not Disturb* sign and opened the doors to the hotels where he has spent a lifetime.

It never really crossed my mind that there was another world beyond the gilded bedrooms, the elegant dining rooms and the well-stocked bars. This was quite often below stairs, as they called it in Victorian times, where the servants and helpers were kept well away from the senior family members, who owned the business, and their guests. This went a stage or two further. In London's finest hostelries there is, indeed, another world and hundreds, sometimes thousands, of workers kept busy ensuring the visitors were properly fed, watered and tucked up in the finest Egyptian cotton sheets, with almost every imaginable whim – including some beyond the imagination of normal folk – catered for.

Imagine a graceful snow-white swan gliding down the Avon, past the Royal Shakespeare Company on the left, the infamous Dirty Duck public house on the right and on past the church where the venerable Bard, William is laid to rest; all is serene and beautiful above the water, but those little legs and webbed feet are going like the clappers below the surface. That, I now realise after sharing Neil's memories, is what hotel life is truly like.

I doubt there is anyone better equipped than Neil Kirby to reveal that truth, sometimes hilarious, sometimes amazing and occasionally even downright disgraceful, but always absolutely fascinating. A case of who would have thought it. Certainly not me.

With just a ten-minute walk along the glorious Eastbourne front from my Victorian apartment to Neil's almost as old hotel, it was scarcely a chore and not only provided me with something to keep my mind active and stave off dementia, but also gave me a base at the hotel with its spectacular vista of the sea washing over miles and miles of beach. No wonder he says he bought the hotel for the view!

But, enough of me, I want you to meet Neil Kirby who began, literally at the bottom of the pile, a pile of dirty sheets and then washing greasy pots and pans in an underground kitchen, working his way to the very top, managing one of the finest most respected hotels in the world in the heart of London's opulent Mayfair and now the proud owner of his own pile, the century-old Langham Hotel. In this instance you have my permission to ignore the *Do Not Disturb* notice and push open the double doors to a world you scarcely knew existed. Eat your heart out Eliza Doolittle!

Bob Harris

Eastbourne

September 2024

Contents

Introduction	By Bob Harris	v
CHAPTER 1	My Old Man	2
CHAPTER 2	Run, Neil, Run	12
CHAPTER 3	Wendy, My One True Love	32
CHAPTER 4	Profitt And Loss!	38
CHAPTER 5	Do Not Disturb	52
CHAPTER 6	The Good, Bad And The Covid	58
CHAPTER 7	The Customer Is Not Always Right	64
CHAPTER 8	The Long And Winding Road	72
CHAPTER 9	And On To Eastbourne	84
CHAPTER 10	I Do Like To Be Beside The Seaside	105
CHAPTER 11	We Bought It For The View	118
CHAPTER 12	The World At War	128
CHAPTER 13	Life At The Langham	144
CHAPTER 14	Compliments And Complaints	188

Neil Kirby CV

1952 Born in West Kirby, Wirral

1964 Newspaper delivery boy – West Norwood Council Estate

1967 Dorchester Hotel Park Lane – Laundry boy

1967 Grosvenor House Park Lane – Washer up

1967 Grosvenor House Park Lane – Laundry boy

1968 Grosvenor House Park Lane – Valet

1980 Grosvenor House Park Lane – Back of House Manager

1982 Grosvenor House Park Lane – Projects Manager

1984 Grosvenor House Park Lane – Sales & Marketing Executive

1986 Grosvenor House Park Lane – Apartments Manager

1990 Grosvenor House Park Lane – Deputy General Manager

1993 Grosvenor House Park Lane – General Manager

1994 Berystede Hotel Ascot – General Manager

1997 Pennyhill Park Bagshot – General Manager

2000 Royal Horseguards Hotel London – General Manager

2001 South Lodge Hotel Lower Beeding – General Manager

2005 Langham Hotel Eastbourne – Owner

Do Not Disturb

Neil Kirby

DO NOT DISTURB

CHAPTER ONE

MY OLD MAN

My father George summed up everything I loved about the Langham Hotel in Royal Parade, Eastbourne.

My wife Wendy and I had cashed in our life savings – and a bit more besides - to buy this Victorian pile and my dad, at the age of 104, liked nothing better than sitting in the bay window of his private rooms extolling the virtues of his wonderful view.

I always said I bought it for the view but, to Dad, it was more than the sea crashing onto the miles of beaches, sparkling in the East Sussex sunshine in front of the hotel we owned. It was the constant beauty parade of pretty girls in their bikinis and swimsuits, sunbathing and swimming.

My dad, George, was, as you can probably already guess, something of a character and became a worldwide personality when he and his paramour Doreen were married in front of the world's press, cameras and radio with a combined age of 194!

This all took place in the Langham Hotel on 13 June 2015, when they became the oldest couple in the world to marry, making their way into the Guinness Book of Records. Their wedding day was also his 103rd birthday, while his wife Doreen was a sprightly 91. They were together for a total of 30 years until Dad passed away.

The Guinness Book of Records contacted me after their researchers had picked it up from the local and national press and asked had I realised they were the oldest couple to wed in the world, when their joint years were added together.

Guinness had come to know about the nuptials when the then prime minister, David Cameron, was on a visit to Eastbourne. Our local

Member of Parliament, Caroline Ansell, was told about the wedding and came to visit with all the attendant hoo-hah in the national press.

Mr Cameron broke off a meeting with Caroline, saying he wanted to meet George and Doreen himself. They were both Conservatives, so there was no problem there, and it was arranged for the MP and PM to visit the hotel.

Cameron was introduced to us, much to the delight of Wendy who thought he was a good looking chap. Dad was sitting in an easy chair in the hotel bar with the politicians. The introductions were made, with Dad clearly wondering what the hell was going on with the fuss and the camera flashes and lots of folk he did not know.

The photographers, with not a lot of encouragement from Dad, but plenty from the politicians, eventually set up a group photograph with the Prime Minister sat casually on the floor by the side of Dad, who had his hand on Cameron's shoulder, waiting for the pictures to be taken. Suddenly Dad turned to him and said: "Who are you?"

Cameron rode it well and told him who he was, to which Dad said to him: "Let me tell you something, you've got dirty shoes." It brought the house down and both Cameron and Caroline fell about laughing, taking it in the right spirit from an old serviceman.

The Prime Minister subsequently sent a delightful letter to Dad wishing him well on his wedding day. The big day itself was exactly that, with media attracted from all over the world… China, America, much of Europe, represented by photographers, TV cameramen, commentators and scribblers. We had a wonderful reception for some sixty people in our hotel restaurant. A day to remember.

Do Not Disturb

VIP guests local MP Caroline Ansell and the then Prime Minister David Cameron celebrate George and Doreen's forthcoming wedding, George 103 and Doreen 91 years old, the oldest couple (joint ages) in the world to marry earning them a place in the Guinness Book of Records.

I was very proud to be his best man and we both wore blue suits and pink ties. When we cremated Dad, we dressed him in his wedding suit with the pink tie. I often wear my pink tie when I'm doing talks on my life in hospitality, now 57 years. I talk about him in my presentation with pictures of the wedding on a large screen, so he is always in my thoughts.

My sister Sandra was always there to help Dad and Doreen. As my dad used to say "She's my favourite of all my kids, she's a good'un" and he was right. She always came to see him and Doreen at the hotel and when they lived in Staplehurst in Kent and Cornwall. We all knew it was tough for Doreen looking after Dad, washing and dressing him every day so I was pleased when they came to live with us at the Langham. They were so happy living here during their last years, with maid service and meals in the restaurant, they deserved it.

Dad was born in Buckingham Palace Road in London, where his parents managed a public house called The Victoria, and they always boasted that their nearest neighbour was the King of England. A true statement because there were no other buildings at the time between the Vic and Buck House. He was born upstairs in the original pub, which is long gone and now a block of offices. It was June 1912, two months after the Titanic sank.

Indeed, one of their regular customers was the Prince of Wales, who would use the saloon bar where you paid a bit more for your pint of ale or your glass of porter than in the public bar where the riff raff hung out. Dad's parents fell out, separated and got divorced, with his father running off with another woman while his wife left The Victoria and took over The Plough at Clapham, along with the four brothers and a sister for help and support.

He went through his school years where he excelled in boxing, winning all his 60 fights and becoming Imperial Services champion. He joined the Royal Navy at 14 in 1926, lying about his age. Thirteen years later, when war broke out, he and two of his brothers, Ernie and Eddie, went off to defend the country, leaving the youngest boy,

Frank, at home with his sister. The bombs were dropping over London and Clapham, where the family home was, and they suffered along with everyone else.

One day during the Blitz the sirens went wild. Instead of going to the air raid shelter, Dad's sister and a friend went down into the basement when a bomb hit the side of the house. Frank, who had gone into the proper shelter on his way home from school, found his sister and her friend dead when the all-clear sirens sounded. The bomb didn't kill them, but it had broken the gas pipe, and they were trapped and eventually overcome by the fumes and died.

Dad had come out of the Navy before the Second World War after five years' service. Because promotion was slow in the navy, he joined the RAF where he was a physical instructor. He was quite a renowned fighter and had two of his title fights at the Royal Albert Hall, watched by the future King, Edward VIII, a keen fan, who hadn't seen him lose a fight and who presented him with a personally signed leather book, congratulating him.

What a family heirloom that would have been had it been looked after and saved, along with his solid silver trophies. I didn't see them but Frank, who used to come to the hotel to see Dad, said they were a beautiful sight. The real tragedy followed the deaths of his sister and her friend, when thieves raided the bombed houses and stole anything they could carry off. Frank told me looters were rife, everywhere. They stole the leather book, which they probably binned, and almost certainly had the silver trophies melted down. I never saw a single trophy and only had a picture, which one of my brothers kept.

To compensate I have pictures of Dad and Doreen in the bar at the hotel, pictured as the oldest couple in the world to marry.

Neil Kirby

George and Doreen with Guinness World Record Certificate as the oldest couple to marry with an aggregate age of 194 years 280 days.

Working long hours and bringing up a young family, I didn't see him regularly as I would have liked. I count my blessings that Wendy and I were able to look after him for eight years in the Langham. That meant an awful lot to me, as did being with him when he passed on.

Eddie died first, followed by Ernie, but Frank survived and lived until he was 97, and was at my father's wedding at the hotel.

I loved my dad, he was my hero, but by Frank's account he was nasty to his brother at times, particularly when he came back from the forces and used to hit him with his swagger stick. He struggled with nightmares, which Frank remembered, and he would hear him fighting people in his dreams. Dad being a physical man, wanted to fight, and he became frustrated that he was forced to stay at home and prepare those going into battle. When I spoke to Frank about it, he was very forgiving, pointing out that he had all those fights, lost his sister, his favourite in the family, and was frustrated at not being able to go to the front and fight the enemy.

He was married before he met mum. Apparently his first wife was considerably older than him and was comparatively well off, living in her home in Streatham. They had no children and when he met my mum he fell in love with her body and her mind in that order and they went off together. Easy come, easy go.

He retired at 65 and started work as a gardener. He worked until he was 92, advertising for work in magazines and papers, meeting a few nice ladies from Purley along the way when he tended their plots of land.

He became very proficient, picking up his trade as he went along and attending lectures at night school. He knew all the Latin names of the flowers and even designed gardens himself. It sounds very grand, but they were small gardens, and he was probably on about five pounds an hour, cash in hand. He did it for many years but four hip replacements, two hips done twice, restricted him somewhat, as they were made like Meccano sets in those days, whereas my replacement hip is titanium and should last, I hope, for twenty years. Because he was shovelling and raking in his job there was a lot of hip movement, and they would only last for six or seven years before they needed replacing.

He was a great guy and even though he hit his youngest brother with a stick, we put that down to frustration. He never hit me or any of my other brothers and sisters, ever. He could have done. When I was washer upper and laundry boy, I would occasionally steal half a crown out of his top drawer to pay for my bus fare and something to eat. I confessed what I had done when he was living with me in the Langham when he was past his one hundredth birthday. He told me that he knew, and that I was a little you-know-what. But I was glad I told him, it got something off my chest that had lingered there for a long while.

I still have pictures of him when we lived in the halfway house at Battersea. We always looked to be having such fun, in the park on his shoulders or in a rowing boat on the lake. He was a nice, kind man and never looked for trouble.

He was a remarkable fellow when he came to live with us at the hotel, and although he had to admit he was not as fit as he was, he was still strong of mind until his dying day, never needing a hearing aid and only wearing glasses to read. His room in the Langham Hotel, where he and Doreen lived, overlooked the sea and he loved to just sit there in his bay window, watching those girls in their bikinis and swimsuits.

Nothing unusual, other than the fact he was 104 at the time! The night before he died, he was as active as ever. Doreen was entertaining a cousin of hers in the dining room while I looked after him in his room. He wasn't as strong as he used to be, regressing from a stick to help him walk, then onto to a Zimmer frame and finishing up in a wheelchair. He always used to tell me to keep my legs strong and that once they were gone you were on the downward slope. I have followed his advice all my life, running thousands of miles and competing in races round the country and abroad.

Do Not Disturb

The night before he passed away he fretted about where his wife was and what she was doing, so I distracted him by sorting out his dinner from room service. He wanted tomato soup and a piece of halibut along with a couple of glasses of the sweet German wine he preferred, Liebfraumilch. His other tipple was a large gin and tonic.

It was a summer evening and we sat in the window watching the last of the sunbathers with him pointing out the girls with the biggest breasts. While he ogled the array of beauty, there was a rap on the door as a pretty new waitress brought in his soup. Sharp as ever he asked her what her name was and when she told him it was Cats, he laughed and said he'd never heard anything like it, and then told her to get her clothes off and get into bed!

I was mortified and told him he couldn't say things like that to the staff or, indeed, anyone else at his age. "I can say whatever I want," he said, "So come on, get your clothes off." She went all pink and flustered, while I explained he was my dad and was only teasing her.

What can you say to a man of 104 about not chatting up the birds? Not a lot. I went to bed chuckling that night and was helping with the breakfasts at around 7.30am the next morning when I received a call telling me that Doreen had phoned down to say that Dad had a little fall, nothing unusual, and I said I would be straight up.

When I arrived, I found him in the bathroom on the floor and I knew straight away that we had lost him. We did what we could, called an ambulance and four medics turned up in the blink of an eye. But even at that stage I knew it was a lost cause. The medics worked desperately because they thought they detected a weak heartbeat, but I could have told them that he had a pacemaker fitted when he was 94, ten years earlier, and this was what they could hear.

They ripped open his pyjamas and set to work on him, trying to revive him. I sat on a chair watching, knowing that they were brave attempts, but futile. They must have tried for twenty minutes until a fifth medic arrived and told them to stop and that there was nothing from the heart, only from the pacemaker. I told the story at the crematorium about his last night and his cheeky flirtation with the girl. Everyone laughed because they knew what he was like.

Doreen carried on living with us after his death. We had prepared for this eventuality by making sure they were wed, making her a fully-fledged Kirby. Her daughter had sadly died and her granddaughter didn't have much contact with her. A year later Doreen suffered a stroke and was paralyzed all down one side. She was taken to the local hospital in Eastbourne, but there was little they could do for her, and she was transferred to a nearby care home where she lived for another three years. She suffered a second stroke and died peacefully in the home aged 98, four years after Dad who died in 2016, a year after they married.

We used to joke that he had the Do Not Disturb sign on his door for his year of marriage because they were always at it. His response was: "Bloody well wish it was true."

CHAPTER TWO

RUN, NEIL, RUN

I was born on 15 November 1952, in the RAF Barracks, Wirral in West Kirby, where my dad George Victor Ernest Kirby, served his country. I went back there some years ago and all the barracks had been torn down apart from the block of houses where I was born and were then private residences, leaving just a stone with the inscription *RAF Barracks Kirby* as the sole reminder of the past. I do not know if they still stand because I couldn't bring myself to return. Nothing to see here, move along please.

We weren't there long in any case, and after two years dad was transferred to RAF Bruggen in West Germany for the next four years where a great deal happened to shape my future life.

I had the misfortune to be born bowlegged, so bad you could see the east coast through my legs when I stood up anything but straight. I kept falling over because my legs were so bowed, and it was soon decided that they needed to operate to straighten them before I was too much older. It was not as if I was skinny or anything, in fact I was 11lbs when I was born and like a baby gorilla. I was put in plaster from hips to feet by the English doctors on the base and had special boots made for me, not that I could do any walking in them. I was so plastered I couldn't even drag myself to the toilet, as I couldn't bend my legs. But the plaster was better than callipers, so everyone told me.

They also made me a special table, something we kept for thirty years before it was unfortunately discarded. This was for when I went to the loo, I sat on the throne with my legs straight out in front of me on the table because I couldn't manipulate my legs. They were not painful, just a little uncomfortable, caused by sores which itched like hell and the only relief I could get was by sticking a knitting needle down the plaster and giving it a good scratch.

The plaster was changed every six months during the two years I wore it. I was four years of age and desperate to run about with the other kids and it was a terrible indignity, but eventually all the effort was worthwhile. Thanks to those clever, inventive doctors in Bruggen, I went on to run many a marathon with legs as perfect as you could wish. But for those medics who didn't want me shipped back to England, I would not have grown up to play football, run and do all the other things that most people take for granted.

We returned to England in 1958 when dad came out of the RAF and went to live in Wolverhampton, where two of his brothers, Frank and Ernie, resided. There were all sorts of family feuds and Mum didn't like it there at all, even though we were in a brand new house, a lovely place, detached, three bedrooms and bright red garage doors, a useful storage area as we had no car.

It couldn't last because of the simmering feud with some of the family and so Dad sold the house, and we moved south to Battersea, alongside the landmark Battersea Power Station in the south of the capital. Dad had done a deal with a builder in Clapham and with four kids in the family already, needed to change the layout of the house to accommodate all six of us. The alterations were started by the builders only for my dad to pull out of the deal. I was too young to know what it was all about, but Dad was taken to court, and he ended up with not much of the money left from his demob payment and the sale of the Midlands house.

From London we moved to Bognor Regis, a marvellous place for us kids to live and the house dad rented was, to us, a mansion. We lived there for a year renting and surviving on his pension, until that ran out as well. He tried everywhere for a decent job, but men were flocking back after national service, coming out of the services like him during decolonisation with no qualifications and not knowing what to do.

He was a sergeant, an instructor and a boxer, teaching the recruits how to stab an enemy and how to survive when they were parachuted into enemy territory. It was all very SAS before the specialist units were formed but it did little to find him a permanent occupation and he was reduced to odd jobs, like gardening and driving.

Do Not Disturb

One of my most strident memories of dad at the time was him going into a pub with his brother, to celebrate Ernie being home on leave from the tank regiment and all four of them enjoying a drink. Dad went to the toilet and when he came back three drunken bums were hassling one of the brothers. Dad took them outside and gave them a beating. He came back without a scratch.

He used to tag them under the jaw, and they always fell. He taught me and I had 11 fights myself without a defeat and always followed his sage advice, and still do! Brother Frank said he had never seen anything like it. He had watched dad box competitively but had never seen him in a roughhouse and couldn't believe the way he handled himself and put down all three like John Wayne in the movies.

After Bognor when the money ran out, we ended up in a halfway house back in Battersea in 1960, with rats as big as cats while dad, who was not allowed to stay with us, had to find a cheap bed and breakfast and try to find himself a full time job.

We were stuck in this disgusting hovel for six months with horrible neighbours all sleeping cheek by jowl in a dormitory alongside rats and with no money. It was like a Charles Dickens novel. The food consisted of things like tripe and pig's trotters, bread and dripping, followed by bread and butter pudding, sometimes minus the butter! The rats thrived better than we did because we were next to a glucose factory.

We all used to attend the huge Victorian bathhouse down the road every Friday, with a towel and a bar of soap, because of the lack of any sort of facilities in the two flats we had been allocated. They were called, would you believe, Magnolia Mansions. We used to enjoy our bath in individual cubicles with dad patrolling outside and shouting through the doors asking if we were okay. He was given the usual six months to find a job before we were all kicked out, regardless of whether this large family had anywhere to live or not. With such a big family there were constant comings and goings and to facilitate the constant ebb and flow, dad attached the front door key to a piece of string which could be pulled through the letter box for easy access.

Our simple plan was rumbled by one of the local villains who let himself in when mum and dad were out at the local. My sister Sandra, then ten, was in bed and when she saw this strange man in her bedroom gave a polite "hello" to the surprised burglar who responded in kind before scuttling off with his ill-gotten gains.

There wasn't much to steal but he took whatever was portable and worth a few bob, including a wall clock that my father had been awarded during his boxing career. I assume the fool who took it couldn't read, because had he been able, he would have seen the inscription "Imperial Services Boxing Champion" and would have kept his distance. My dad thought he would be back because it had been so easy for him. Sure enough, this half-wit returned, pulled the key through the letter box, let himself in and walked straight into an uppercut to his jaw from Dad, which laid him out cold.

Dad was the instant hero, congratulated by the neighbours who had been plagued by this gormless burglar and even was given a pat on the back by the police. How times have changed, nowadays it would have been dad in trouble for daring to lay a finger on a crook, caught in the act of breaking and entering.

We were then moved to York Hill Council estate in West Norwood where we were housed in a four bedroom flat on the third floor. This was where I lived for five or six years from the age of nine while Dad at last had a full time job at Advance Laundries in Camberwell as assistant manager looking after the big machines that, among other things, washed the bedding from the grand hotels. Something which was to play a large part in my future. I visited it when I was young and was amazed at the size of everything, especially the huge rollers used for pressing. The floor was always awash with puddles of water and the car park was constantly filled with big trucks bringing in and taking away the hampers of laundry.

I started at Fenstanton Primary School, in Tulse Hill. We were in a nice, clean council estate where I quickly made friends with kids of my own age, joining the cubs where I became a "sixer" with a couple of yellow stripes on the sleeve of my uniform, heading my own little group of six kids. Every year we used to do the famous 'Bob a Job' week, going round people's houses, knocking on the door and saying "Bob a Job". I would sweep the driveway, cut back weeds in gardens, clean their car, all for the Cubs charity of the week. I loved it. I stole half a crown from the money given to me, well I had to eat and drink while doing all their chores!

School, however, was not so much fun due to my dyslexia, an unknown word and condition to me and the rest of the family, and I was blamed and castigated for achieving poor test results. It was years before my handicap was recognised and named.

Not the greatest of starts to my young life with my bow legs and then my dyslexia but, thanks to the RAF doctors, I was finally up, running and into the same mischief as every other lad of my age, both then and now. Trouble followed me, and hide-and-seek seemed like a good idea as we chased each other across a factory roof until I tripped and fell through the wired glass roof of the Nestle's ice cream factory.

I tumbled a good fifty feet and found myself covered in glass and blood. My mates had seen what had happened and were scared to death, they bolted homewards, leaving me to my fate. Apart from my wounds and injured pride, I discovered that as it was Sunday the factory was locked and secured with not a soul around to help me.

I did find a ladies' toilet where I was able to wash away some of the blood and then climbed a flight of stairs and discovered a barred window looking out on the flats where I lived. I managed to squeeze through the bars and let myself drop the thirty feet to the ground without doing myself any further damage and made my way home. My horrified mother tried to clean me up but when she found a deep gash under my arm caused by the wired glass, she promptly passed out and dad took over. He rushed me to the local hospital where it took them four hours and 32 stitches, cleaning the rust off my wounds and putting me back together. Remarkably, despite the two long drops, nothing was broken, but I still have the scars under my arm to this day to remind me of what could have been a far more serious accident. But it is what kids do.

From primary school I went to Kingsdale School in Dulwich when I was 11. This was smart. It was a modern building opened only five years earlier. The architect was Leslie Martin who had designed the Royal Festival Hall. The school were proud of the connection, but I doubt it was something he was gratified with, as the classrooms were separated by very narrow corridors without windows, perfect for the school bullies to exercise their authority over the smaller, weaker children.

It was not something that concerned me then and I remember rocking up in my blazer and my cap, carrying my little satchel, only to be told I had arrived a day too early and to come back the next day! Mum had sent me in on inset day when the teachers gathered to plot the term ahead. I was not bothered and having seen it, I was all the keener to return the next day, especially as it was only a single stop on the train and a mile walk.

I wasn't the most attentive pupil and got more pleasure from looking out of the classroom window at the girls in their blue knickers and short skirts, playing netball and rounders. It got me into trouble when the teacher asked whether I was listening, and I would answer no, because I was watching the girls. I used to get stressed that I couldn't write like the other kids and my concentration was never good. I was also having difficulties hearing and it was finally agreed there was something wrong. I was taken to see a doctor to have my ears syringed and within a week I was in hospital having my tonsils and adenoids removed.

Mum tried to soften the blow by telling me they would serve ice cream every day and they might have done in the children's ward, but I was put in an adult ward where ice cream was not a factor. I had to suffer the sore throat with no vanilla ice to cool it down. But I was soon out and up to mischief with a growing group of mates. For someone who did not like school, I quickly settled in the new environment, not because I was suddenly good at English and maths, but because of the sport.

I was cross-country champion for my age group and went on to become south London champion. I had discovered something I really loved. Running. It was the freedom, and I was good at it, a far cry from those days when my legs were in plaster in Germany. I took part in the All England Cross Country Championships in Sheffield and then I ran in Derby and was picked to race in the London Schools mile. My fitness and athleticism also helped when we began playing football, another sport which came naturally to me, helped by my speed and stamina built up over the cross country courses.

I not only made the school team but was also scouted by both Charlton and my local team Crystal Palace. I had my first girlfriend when I was twelve at Kingsdale School which also required my developing athleticism. To meet up with her I had to walk to the station, get a train to Gypsy Hill and then another to Dulwich, followed by another walk. She was a year older than me and lived in Brockley by Millwall's ground, the Den. On one date with her I had spent all my pocket money, and I had no train or bus fare to get home. So, I decided to run, something I was doing and enjoying regularly, with a 4 minute 36 second mile and the South London mile title under my belt. What was a run across London compared to that? Nothing! I was wearing jeans and trainers but hadn't a clue of the directions I should take. I kept going wrong and by this time it was approaching midnight and my parents were having kittens wondering where I was. There were no mobile phones, of course, and dad and my brothers set out to try and find me. I got back before them and was in all sorts of trouble. It didn't put me off and we went out for a couple of years on and off including a two week trip to Sayers Croft in Surrey on a school holiday before she dumped me.

I was, however, playing football, a game I fell in love with instantly and kicked a ball or whatever around every spare minute. School held no interest apart from the sport, the girls and history, one subject I enjoyed. I was constantly on detention and would bunk off whenever the opportunity presented itself. If I went home mum would ask me what I was up to and when I told her, she would just tell me to do the washing up. Mum and dad were still together then but not really together, with mum expecting a fifth child, reputedly fathered by the local bingo caller. On its own number five, then Tom Mix, number six, probably by the same father, with mum now aged 46. A full house you might say.

I heard all sorts of unsavoury stories including from one of my siblings, that Dad used to pay Mum for the privilege of having sex. How sad was that? It was a small flat with a lot of people and everything was an open book. She was a good mum to the kids and very kind. They went through some terrible times but neither of them ever hit me. I put their eventual separation down to the problems we had in Battersea and thereafter with the shortage of money. We were so short of cash that a treat for Dad would be to take an empty bottle to the off licence and have it filled with cheap wine out of the barrel and on the way home he would buy himself a few pence worth of winkles from the mobile fishmonger's cart.

For Mum it was her beloved bingo, always hoping for the big prize, and her fifty fags a day. Like Dad, Mum knew how to look after herself and when two young men, both aged in their twenties, started pushing me around and throwing my tennis ball over a fence, she forgot about her trip to the bingo and slapped the biggest one across the face.

Dad arrived at that very moment, and I explained what happened in excited detail. He asked the pair which one had thrown my ball over the fence and the culprit aggressively owned up and asked what he was going to do about it. Big mistake, Dad took off his jacket and put down his cockles and wine somewhere safe and rolled up his sleeves. By now the sideshow had attracted a fair size crowd, who were well aware of these two bullies on the estate. I was worried, as I had never seen my dad fight and with the huge difference in age and height, I was scared he was going to get hurt. I needn't have worried. He offered the boy first shot and gracefully swayed to one side as the roundhouse slid past his chin and Dad threw left, right, left, in a blink of an eye, each one exploding on the chin, knocking the lad out cold. He didn't even bother with the second lad, just telling him to pick up his mate and never to come back to our estate again. The watching crowd were first stunned and then delighted as they broke into spontaneous applause with Dad becoming an instant hero. He was my knight in shining armour.

The rickety marriage might have survived had we moved earlier to the Roundshaw council estate on the old Purley aerodrome, where we had a nice terraced house with a little garden. There were eight of us by now, but although Dad moved with us, he was not always at home and was living his own life.

I carried on with my boxing, training at the famous Thomas a Becket pub in the Old Kent Road, home of so many great British boxers, including Henry Cooper. I caught the eye as a twelve-year-old, boxing the mandatory maximum of three rounds, winning all my 11 fights with no fear.

My dad said that he had heard I was doing a bit of boxing and asked me to show him what I could do. He went off to fetch his gloves, which I had never seen and were kept in a metal box under the stairs. He opened it up and took out his old sparring gloves and we squared off in the kitchen, to see if I was any good. It didn't take him long to decide I wasn't, and that was it. I hung up my gloves before I had any. It was probably the only time I had listened to my father, and I was easily swayed because I was now so much into football. I didn't want my nose broken again. You get hurt more sparring than fighting and I had it broken eight times.

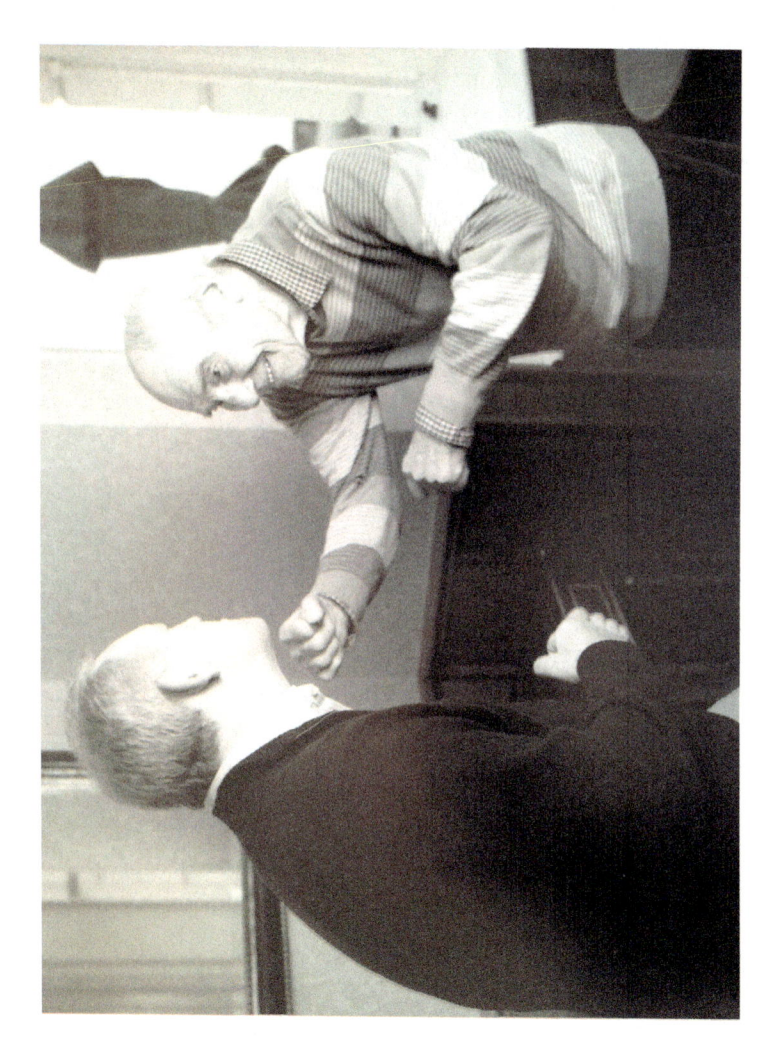

Father George lands right cross on Neil's chin as they celebrate Dad's century.

Do Not Disturb

I was 15 when we moved to the Roundshaw Estate in Purley just down the road from Crystal Palace Football Club. It was there that I began my working life, like many kids of my age around the country, delivering newspapers. With my legs straightened and working well, I had taken to football and was spotted by Crystal Palace chairman Arthur Rowe when I was captaining my school team in the Surrey Schoolboys final. He invited me to join them for training sessions after watching me score a couple of goals.

I explained that I was already with Charlton Athletic, along with one of my teammates but that I was keen to switch. I was delighted at their interest, because I was fed up with travelling into London and out again by train on my own, aged just 11. When we got there the training ground was the car park, not a place where you developed your sliding tackle! There were no well-equipped private grounds then as there are now with luxurious facilities for training, playing, showering and eating.

Palace were quickly able to sort out the necessary paperwork and they were pleased when they discovered I was local and invited me to go along to the ground where I signed a young players contract, trained with them, acted as ball boy for the senior games at Selhurst Park and eventually became an apprentice when I attained the age of 15. I enjoyed my time and was pleased when manager Bert Head wanted me to sign as an apprentice professional on a three month contract to see whether I was good enough.

The truth is, I wasn't and after three months they let me go. I enjoyed it there alongside players like John Jackson and Mark Lazarus, lovely people and when I left Palace, I played my football at a decent level for clubs like Beckenham Town and Whyteleafe and really enjoyed the experience.

I still occasionally see Stevie Kember, whose boots I used to clean. He did rather better than me with Palace. Not so long ago he came to the Langham with his brother for a Masonic ladies' festival and we reminisced and had our photograph taken together. Another player from my brief Palace days was Nicky Chatterton, who lives up the road from the Langham. His dad was groundsman and I used to clean Nicky's boots as well, all good practice for when I went to work as a valet at Grosvenor House.

Nicky was at the club from a youngster for 21 years. I played with him at youth level but then he developed, while I was shown the door. He stayed for a while at Palace where he made 151 first team appearances before moving to their local rivals Millwall where he had a further 264 games for the old enemy and finished his career at Colchester. I only discovered we were neighbours when I bumped into his wife while out running and she told me her name was Chatterton and it transpired he was living not far away in Eastbourne. Small world.

I carried on playing at a decent level until I was coming up to my thirties. Then, one day, my knee started swelling and I missed a cup final and I became concerned it would affect my running. I was never happier than when I was in my shorts, singlet and trainers pounding the streets. Like Forest Gump I could run all day and not get out of breath or tired.

I might have left south London, but south London has never left me. Although I may have been brought up in "Souf London" rather than within the sound of Bow Bells of St Mary-le-Bow in the East End, Cockney rhyming slang was still very much part of the culture of a young man growing up in the capital, especially around the hotels where I worked my passage for 28 years.

Nowadays it is heard more on television programmes than in the streets, but none of regulars at the Langham are in any doubt where my origins lie, and I am not averse to baffling them with a bit of rhyming slang for good effect. It is much more polite to call an idiot "a banker" instead of "a wanker" and have him deny he works in a bank!

I do it to confuse my staff as well, asking them what they are doing wearing white almond rocks instead of black. That's another of my little pet hates, wearing white socks (almond rocks) with black daisy roots (boots) and black Callard and Browsers (trousers). I'll ask them what they are doing with their dog and bone instead of leaving it in the locker room. "Dog and bone?" they ask, looking baffled. Mobile phone – and the point is made with a smile instead of a sharp word. Or I might say to one of the cleaners that someone has had a right old tommy tit in the toilets, and can they clean it up. That doesn't take a lot of working out!

Rhyming slang remains an ongoing and up to date, and even the Coronavirus became known as Miley Cyrus (a case of the Miley's), while other little examples are; Claire Rayner's, trainers; Britney Spears, beers; Catherine Zeta-Jones, moans and Myleen Klass ... well, you get the idea.

When Palace kicked me out when I was 15, my dad told me to start working for a living in 1967. Dad, being manager of the laundry company who had all the contracts for the major hotels, got me working first at the Dorchester Hotel, catching the dirty sheets and towels when they were thrown down the chutes to the basement. The laundry company used to be paid to send their own staff to count and collect the items that needed laundering. I did it for three weeks, counting the dirty sheets, putting them in the hampers and dragging them to be washed, using a large metal hook. It didn't faze me. I was tough enough to look after myself and everyone always thought I was older than I was, although I was caught out in the bookmakers when placing a shilling each way on a horse, when the cashier told me in no uncertain terms to sling my hook. Trying to look grown up, I had walked in with a filter ciggy in my mouth but hadn't noticed I had it the wrong way round.

That first job at the Dorchester lasted for a fortnight before Dad sent me to see a friend of his who got me a job washing up at the Grosvenor House in 1967. I was good at it, diligent but hated every minute of it. The conditions were nothing like today, with the stainless steel sinks and the sophisticated machinery. It was back breaking, hard work and up to our armpits in greasy bubbles in a huge metal sink.

There was no conveyer belt with everything having to be moved by hand. The worst were the frying pans which were thick with grease. We had to scrape it out with our bare hands, sling the muck in the bin so that you didn't block the drains before scrubbing it until it sparkled. I slaved away there for about six months, then to the laundry for a further six months before finally being promoted to valet and the real beginning of my career in hotels.

My running career started in 1982 when I entered the Burnham Beeches Half Marathon. I had watched the first London Marathon in 1981 and decided that was something I would like to do. I finished the half marathon in 1 hour 28 minutes and from then on, I was hooked.

I started training five times a week and signed up for the Manchester Piccadilly Marathon with some colleagues from Grosvenor House, which I completed in 3 hours 14 minutes. I told Wendy I would be finishing in around 4 hours but when I got to the finish line she was nowhere to be seen. I was freezing and asked the organiser to announce over the loudspeaker that I was waiting for her. It turned out she was in the pub with our friends, not expecting me for another three quarters of an hour! My colleague and I raised £1,800 for Great Ormond Street Children's Hospital and we had to present the cheque to Sir Jimmy Saville and I still have the photograph to prove it, although that's not something I like to publicise too much nowadays!

I love running. It helps my stress levels. After a good run I feel so much better, my mind is so much clearer. I think about the business and it helps me plan for the future, sales growth, saving costs and wages. I think through where we are week by week, month by month, sales growth or sales not growing, make changes to staff, how I can make savings. I look at how we can improve our room rate, increase when we are busy, reduce when we are quiet. All when I am out running, I come back with a focus and new ideas how we will increase sales and how we will make savings, and most importantly how to improve customer service.

Running keeps me fit. I don't take any tablets at my age of 72 years this year. Fitness is so important to me like my father who lived to 104 years old. I want to live till I'm 106! I will be trying to beat the 100 metre record for the over 100 years olds'. I think last time I looked it was 32 seconds. I'm up for that and most importantly to raise money for charities.

In 1987 I was working at Grosvenor House and we were living in Sanderstead when the Great Storm struck overnight on 15th-16th October. We awoke to find chaos. Incredibly, the whole family had slept through the whole thing! The country had come to a standstill, with trees blown down blocking roads and railway lines so no buses or trains. I had to cut down a tree that had fallen blocking our driveway, thinking I would be able to drive to work but no chance. All the local roads and roads going into London were blocked. I had to get to Grosvenor House because half of the staff weren't able to get to work. So I put on my running gear, rucksack on my back, said goodbye to the family, not sure when I'll be back. I ran down to the A23 and into Croydon, through Thornton Heath, Norbury, Streatham Common, Brixton, Vauxhall and Victoria, finishing in Park Lane. 15 miles distance in 1 hour 55 minutes. Didn't get back home for four days as many staff were still unable to get to work so had to help making beds, serving food, etc.

I remember when I was at the Langham early on this guy came in and stole a bottle of beer from the bar. The staff called me and told me what had happened. I came out of my office and saw this young lad run out of the bar via the terrace. He was about 50 yards in front of me so I ran after him. He kept turning round, making a rude gesture and shouting "Come on old fellow, keep up!" I wasn't going to give in so I kept running. After 600 yards he still kept shouting "Come on old man!" but what he didn't know was that I was a long distance runner. So slowly I began to catch up with him. He couldn't believe I was still there, slowly closing the gap. Then I was right there and grabbed him round the neck "Got you you f****** b******!, thought you could steal from me did you?" I had him in a headlock and marched him back to the hotel and through the bar. All the guests who had seen what happened gave me a standing ovation! It was as if I was a hero.

While my staff called the police, I took him down into the kitchen and, out of view of the guests, as he was still shouting at me to let him go, I "accidentally" banged his head against the wall. "Oops sorry" I said. Police arrived and arrested him. Taught him a lesson not to mess with me or steal my property. Never saw him again!

Another time a young lad thought he would steal a bottle of beer from the bar. As I ran after him, I saw him jump onto a bike and pedal off down the seafront. I got a good look at him, remembering his white shoes, clothes he was wearing and his face. I never panic in those situations, just jumped into my car and drove down the road looking for this guy on his bike. Half a mile down the road I saw him on the right hand side sitting on a bench with a girl, looking out to sea. So I parked up slowly and walked along the front very casually, minding my own business. As I got alongside him, I grabbed him, pushed him to the ground and sat on him holding his hands so he couldn't punch me. Looking into his eyes I said "Don't even think about trying to escape or I'll break your arm". I asked a passerby to call the police and they arrived very quickly, cuffed him and took him away. Never saw him again either!

One morning I got a phone call from my Night Manager. "Hi Boss, the beer company came this morning and took five barrels of lager and draught beer. I helped them put them on the van."

"What beer company? Who were they?"

"Oh it was just a plain white van Boss, don't know what company it was. They came at 5.45 this morning. Said they were taking the beer away because it was out of date".

"Well, you've been conned! You should have rung me to check before you helped the conmen steal £700 worth of beer!"

To date I have run 52 marathons, including 19 London Marathons, four 50k and one 50 mile ultramarathons, 223 half marathons and many other shorter distances, raising a total of £385,000 over the years.

Do Not Disturb

In November 2022 I broke the world record for the first over 70 year old to run a marathon on a treadmill in 4 hours 24 minutes. We hired two treadmills which were installed on the terrace of the Langham under a gazebo. To become a world record we had to have two adjudicators to sign off that I had completed the race and two independent witnesses in this case the Mayor of Eastbourne and a professional football referee living in Eastbourne. The whole race had to be filmed and sent off to the International World Record Breakers Club based in Berlin. We also raised £8,000 for St Wilfrid's Hospice through sponsorship from the local community.

I have worked out in the 43 years I have been training and racing I have run a total of around 100,000 miles, equivalent to running four times around the world. No wonder I had to have a new hip four years ago! I'm pleased to say I was able to get back running four months after my hip replacement operation. Last year I had to have an operation to repair three hernias caused by lifting heavy suitcases and barrels of beer over the years. Once more I was running again within four months of the operation.

As I write this book, I am in training for a second world record for the first over 70 year old to run 50 kilometres on the treadmill on the terrace of the Langham Hotel on Saturday 12th October 2024. There is currently no world record for this as no one else has tried! The starting pistol will be fired at 10am as I aim to raise over £15,0000 for my chosen charity, Formula One legend Sir Jackie Stewart's "Race Against Dementia".

Neil Kirby

Neil on the treadmill outside Langham hotel running full marathon in 4 hours 26 minutes and achieving a World record for over 70's raising £8,000 for St Wilfrid's Hospice.

Do Not Disturb

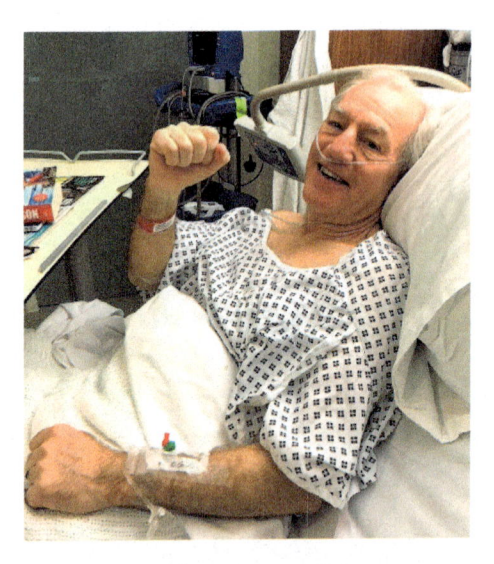

Neil recovering from hip replacement surgery in Princess Grace Hospital February 2020.

Neil and his award after coming first in the Over 60's in the Weald Challenge 50K in 2018.

Like father, like son, they say, and that is certainly true of the Kirbys.

While I'm training for a second world record my son Neil Junior, who spends his life running and organising ultra marathons, is preparing for the Beachy Head 50k in October, an event he was won for the past two years.

He has just come off another major success, winning the famous Race to the Stones, from Lewknor to Lattin Down in Oxfordshire on July 13, when he and fellow running friend Daniel Weller crossed the line side by side, well ahead of the 800 strong field, in the remarkable time of 3: 44: 47, well inside the course record.

Neil is serious about his sport and trains seven days a week, running 90 miles on the South Downs whatever the weather.

We both began our sporting lives as footballers before I discovered that running not only kept me fit but helped relieve stress, while Neil Junior originally ran to keep fit for his favourite sport until he read a book by Dean Karnezes entitled "The Ultramarathon Man" and his life changed. Warning: Be careful what you read!

Since then, he has run and won some of the toughest challenges, especially those around the South Downs area where we both like to train, including winning the South Downs and North Downs Way 100 miles and 50 mile races as well as the Beachy Head 52k, twice.

When he is not training and running, he organises the highly successful UK Ultra trail running events in the South Downs National Park.

Do Not Disturb

CHAPTER THREE

WENDY, MY ONE TRUE LOVE

They say that behind every great man, there's a great woman. It is trite, it is old fashioned, but, in my case, it is a hundred per cent true. My wife Wendy is the love of my life. More than that, much more. Without her I would be a very different Neil Kirby. I doubt I would have enjoyed my fabulous career and I know I would not be a successful hotelier in my own right, acquiring a beautiful Victorian hotel with the best views you could possibly imagine.

Neil and Wendy at Buckingham Palace 2023.

This is the perfect moment in time to celebrate our union for, on 14th September, 2024, we celebrated our Golden Wedding anniversary, 50 years and going as strong as ever.

We met when Wendy was the secretary to Robert Wiles, the apartments manager at the five star Grosvenor House Hotel in Park Lane, London. I had just been promoted from washing the dishes to being a well-dressed valet in a bumblebee outfit, helping to look after the rich and famous from around the globe. It was here that I fell in love with this shy, clever girl who sat in an office behind a desk on one of the floors where I worked. While I came from a council estate in London and spoke with a south London twang, she was a council estate girl who could speak not only English a lot better than me, but also Spanish, German and French. I was instantly taken with this petite, attractive young lady with striking red hair and the shortest of miniskirts and sought out her name: Wendy Golding. I watched her from afar before I plucked up the courage to speak in the staff canteen and saying hello when we passed on the corridor, careful not to be spotted by Mr Wiles, who was also my boss. I discovered that I could make her laugh with my silly jokes, and I soon asked her out for a drink and our relationship developed. We had to be careful because of our work overlapping and we kept our growing relationship a secret, although I have no doubt some of the staff would have spotted us sneaking off for a cuddle and a kiss in one of the empty bedrooms. But I was a proud man in love and wanted everyone to know about it.

I popped the question after eight months and we became engaged in 1973. Her mum and dad, Donald and Winifred, were of the old-fashioned variety and even after a night out together I would have to drive her home from Sutton to Merstham and then drive back again, often nodding off dangerously at the wheel because of my long hours at work.

She was and still is quiet and polite, but very sharp, watching and observing and having an opinion on all she sees.

It has not been wasted, for not only is she my wife, my lover, mother

Do Not Disturb

of my children, my listening post, my support, but also my hard-working joint proprietor at the Langham Hotel, we jointly own in the East Sussex seaside resort of sunny Eastbourne. She mirrors my own attention to detail, spotting a cobweb in the corner of a bedroom, a dud lightbulb to be replaced in a chandelier, a frayed corner in the hall carpet, always looking to make it better for our guests who have to come first. Let's look after the customers, let's make the sales, let's make a profit and put it back into the business, look after the staff – that is still her ethos.

As a result, this hotel, because of the two of us and a dedicated staff, because of our investment of time and money, the tears, the stress and the strain, we have survived and will celebrate our twentieth year at the Langham Hotel on 1st July, 2025. That's something we are both immensely proud of. The marriage has not only survived but flourished, as we are not only best friends, but the co-owners of a successful business. We have our little two-person board meetings everywhere, including the marital bed in our apartment in the hotel, where we permanently live. We talk, we discuss and make decisions together and then she will suddenly decide we should shut ourselves off and concentrate on our own life, our family of three lovely children and seven grandchildren… at the last count.

We have had grief with family bereavements as does everyone no matter what their strata, but there has always been much more joy than sorrow. Wendy is a kind and nice person, some say almost the reverse to me, proving, I suppose, that opposites can attract. I must be hard faced not only with my own staff but with the customers as well, because there is always the odd one who is looking to take advantage of any weakness and to profit from it. To those people who want to damage our trade and our business, I will have no truck. They are out on the street, bags packed and sent looking for another easy mark. But that has to be me and not Wendy, because that is not her style. All the customers like her and love her and I scatter that seed, it is something I encourage, that I am the front man, and she is the brains behind the business – not that she ever offers me any increase in my salary!

She only worked in a hotel once, in an office away from the paying customers, so I have passed on my store of knowledge of how a hotel works and operates, but also how it can fall and fail far quicker than it can reach the summit.

She has learned from me and soaked up all I have to offer but because she is more intelligent than me, she is probably better than me at running the hotel – not that I would ever tell her that. Whereas I draw on my years of experience, she has her background and her brain. She not only knows every aspect of the running of a hotel our size with under 100 rooms, but she also does the VAT, the wages, the National Insurance, the pension schemes, all the hotel's suppliers, secretarial work and then turns her hand to the housekeeping twice a week, making beds, checking arrivals and departures and personally filling in gaps left by days off, sickness and vacancies among the staff.

One day it might be the kitchen and the next rehearsing for our annual pantomime at the hotel, which always a sell out over the half dozen days we put it on, often fully booked by February, and always with a lengthy waiting list.

She is astute and well loved by those who work with her and for her. They know I am the boss at the front of house but, at the same time, they know her place and her value.

But for me she has always been there. When I was at Grosvenor House and had to present budgets, she would do all my typing and put together my reports with me. I would present to her at home the way I was going to do in front of the bosses, and she would tell me to be clearer and more specific, particularly with profit and loss, and to present all the important points slowly and obviously, to give them gravitas. She stopped me waffling and taught me to go for the major points. Instead of sweating and twitching nervously, she showed me how it should be done, the correct words and the pronunciation, which threatened to let me down when I first went from valeting into management.

She has always been fantastically supportive and has helped me grow as a general manager, an owner and as a person. It is not a secure industry, and there were times in my career when I could have been out of the door at any time, and that can produce a tension in any relationship. It is a bit like a football manager: get no results for a year or so and you are out of the door to let someone else in to try. That is often not the basis for a happy and settled marriage and many have failed because of it. Had I not had the unswerving backing of Wendy, who knows what would have happened in my life. I don't think I would have owned a hotel worth well in excess of £3 million with the mortgage paid off any day soon.

She is my backbone, my support, my teacher with my spelling and pronunciation, my rock and my salvation.

We love each other to bits, and we have maintained that level of love for over half a century, even through and after the trials and tribulations of Covid and its dramatic effects on our industry.

Not so long ago I was stressed over a delay in extending our overdraft, not usually a problem with our sound history, but this time it was taken up to the buffers with huge electricity and gas bills to pay along with VAT. I was thinking the worst: having to make staff redundant and all that type of negative thinking. I was even mumbling about it in my sleep and feeling palpitations in my heart. Wendy was aware, a calming influence and right again, because it came through in time and all was well again at the Langham Hotel.

Because we live in and are always available should there be a problem or a catastrophe, we work very long hours, sometimes 19 in a day. However, we can also relax in our apartment, looking out over the sea, because we enjoy each other's company. She makes dinner for us both, she has a glass of Prosecco and maybe I will have a glass of wine, although less often these days, and do the things every happily married couple does. After the pandemic we are looking to loosen up a little and travel more. We started slowly with trips to Jersey and Tenerife but then planned to extend our travel as everyone kept telling me how stressed I looked. Well, thanks a lot, but seriously, there is a need to get away from it all and not think about the place for a week or two. I did for the first ten years, making daily calls when I was away to make certain everything was fine. Now the staff are told only to call me if it is urgent or an emergency. I trust them and let them get on with it. Meanwhile we make up for lost time, walking along a different seafront, going to restaurants for nice meals and meeting new people who don't know what we do for a living. Cruising is another alternative we enjoy and, as ever, we are on the lookout for ideas that will fit into our hotel. It is good to learn from the new generation coming through. Better to see something you like and appreciate than to moan and whinge about a cold steak or a grumpy waiter. Someone else's problem, not ours.

We also go to the shops together and see the good and the bad of the various chain stores where customers don't really matter. The exception for us is our local Sainsbury's in Eastbourne bright, indoor shopping centre where the majority of the staff seem to be in the middle-aged bracket, always friendly and always helpful.

CHAPTER FOUR

PROFITT AND LOSS!

Tips are the lifeblood of the hotel trade, from the liveried doorman who salutes as you enter the five star establishment, right through to the bell boys and chamber maids who cater to the guests every whim and fancy no matter how impossible, demanding or even demeaning. The wages, now as ever, would scarcely be enough to live on, especially those in a capital like London where everything from living, eating and travelling to and from work costs the proverbial arm and a leg.

Don't shed too many tears, because some of those tips can be astronomical and I am not talking about a fiver, a tenner or even a fifty-pound note.

The cash handed out by the sheiks when the black stuff first started gushing out of the sand in the Middle East pales in comparison to the biggest gratuity I was ever given, not by a filthy rich Arab or an American film star, but by a widowed senior citizen from down the road.

It wasn't even when I was working at one of the big London hotels, it was here in Eastbourne in my own hotel overlooking the sea, when a little old lady, who my wife Wendy and I had taken under our wings, left me a staggering and totally unexpected quarter of a million pounds in her will when she passed away.

We knew from experience she was a generous person, for just before the pandemic, in the depths of winter and with trade down, she suddenly presented me with a cheque for £25,000, saying she hoped it would help me and the hotel she loved get through the many problems we were facing.

Of course, both Wendy and I told her that we could not accept such a gift, but she was insistent, saying I would make far more use of it than she could and that it was her way of saying thank you for all we had done for her and it would offend her if we refused.

When we first met Joan Profitt, she was a widow living at the Hawthorns, an upmarket home for the elderly, around a couple of years after we had bought the hotel. We were counting the pennies as we spent fortunes to bring it closer to the standards we wanted; the exterior, the interior, the bedrooms and the public areas all needed refurbishing and improving.

We first met when she came to one of my lunch clubs with a couple of her friends, introduced herself and we immediately struck up a friendship. She also introduced us to her foster daughter Jackie who, it transpired, had an extremely unhappy homelife and Joan and her husband Adrian adopted her, not in the legal sense, but simply and kindly took her into their circle to give her some sort of life.

Joan had previously lived a short way up the road from the hotel in a flat which she was in the process of selling before moving permanently into the Hawthorns, a home she loved. She had a suite there and would often be delighted to repay our hospitality by inviting Wendy and I for lunch, a handy five minutes' drive away. It was far from the sort of care home that afflicts the imagination after bad press and Joan and the other residents were served breakfast, lunch and dinner and lived in some style.

Jackie, then in her fifties, lived in a flat in Lewes. Joan explained that she had gone to the Hawthorns to stay while she had a new kitchen put in and liked it so much, she decided to sell up her own property and make it her permanent home.

Joan became a regular at the Langham, spending Christmas with us and becoming a firm family friend. She liked to cuddle up with me and was, at the same time, great pals with Wendy.

But it came as a complete surprise when, one day, she told me I was looking stressed and asked me what the problem was. I had a good moan, told her I was sick and tired of mounting bills, spending a fortune on refurbishment, and then hitting the inevitable quiet time after Christmas and New Year, when occupancy drops. The same with virtually every hotel in the UK. She promptly said that she would be delighted to help out and give me some money. I laughed and said, of course not, but shortly afterwards she turned up with a cheque made out to Neil and Wendy for £25,000. I asked what it was for, and she replied that it was so that I didn't need to borrow money.

She was adamant that it was not a loan, but a gift and she wanted us both to have it. We argued the toss, but she was insistent and getting upset when she thought we were going to refuse her gesture. We took it and put it in the bank, not using it, ready to hand back if she struck rocky waters. There it sat as our relationship grew until one day she asked as if we would be executors to her will. That was fine, nothing unusual, especially for a lady on her own now that someone she considered to be her foster daughter had sadly passed on with cancer. We helped her out when Jackie died, arranging the funeral and the death certificate, making sure everything was in order. She also asked us to help clear Jackie's flat, which we did, driving her to Lewes to supervise the clearance which was a very emotional experience for her. Jackie was slightly disabled and had help from the government paying for her living quarters. It took two or three days to clear everything up, ferrying the stuff to a charity shop as Joan wanted. We found a couple of thousand pounds in a drawer and lots of new clothes still with their labels on. We asked about it and Joan explained that she had given Jackie an allowance to live on, but she rarely went out and her only vice was smoking and, clearly, shopping for clothes she hardly ever or never wore.

Jackie used to visit Joan once a week, usually on a Friday when they would go to the fish and chip shop for dinner and then come to us and stay for the weekend, especially if it was around a bank holiday time like Easter or Christmas. Jackie would stay for a couple of days and then Joan would put her in a taxi to take her back to her own home.

Jackie left everything in her will to her surrogate mother, not a lot, but enough to pay the funeral costs and the other bits and pieces which come up at such times.

Joan's will was a natural follow up as we took her to her solicitors and made sure it was all done properly. She was well into her eighties and, sadly, she began to suffer with dementia soon afterwards and eventually died just before the pandemic arrived with all its nasty surprises.

I missed her. She used to call me up to a dozen times a day from the Hawthorns, fretting that she hadn't got enough money to pay her bills. I would pop round two or three times a day, just to cheer her up and assure her that there was nothing wrong with her finances. At that time, we didn't know what money she had but knew that her accommodation wasn't cheap, probably around £3,000 to £4,000 a month, including her meals. The home assured us that there were no problems with their payments as we discovered when we helped her sort out her papers. Her husband had been a smart businessman and had left her well looked after with stocks and shares in companies around the world. She had sensibly employed someone to look after the business side for her and when we checked, at her insistence, we were able to assure her that she had around £300,000 in her account. On top of this she had pensions coming in and was clearly not going to suffer financially in any way and we were able to put her mind at rest, until she started worrying about it again a day or two later.

But at least she was able to relax and have a laugh with us and felt properly at home at the Langham.

To settle her nerves and reassure her that all was well, we pinned a sign on the wall in her suite, telling her exactly how much she had in the bank and that there was no hint of financial troubles.

Sadly, the dementia got worse, as it does, and one day we took a call from the Hawthorns to tell us they had found her in midafternoon, in her nightdress lying by the side of her bed. Apparently, she had a fall and hit her head against the radiator. She was rushed to hospital. We dropped everything and went to see her and discovered she had a brain bleed and was in a semi coma. I was annoyed to hear that no one had checked up on her when she failed to appear for breakfast that morning, something she always did, and it was only when she didn't show up for lunch that they finally went to her room to see if there was a problem.

Sadly nothing we could do for her and within a week she had passed away.

Although she had a sister, they never communicated, and it was left to us to arrange her funeral as her executors. The burial was sparsely attended with just myself and Wendy, a few people from the Hawthorns and some of the staff from our hotel, where she was well known and liked.

Her husband was buried over Farnham way and the solicitors told us that she had requested that her ashes be put in his grave with her name added to the headstone.

Then came the bombshell.

The solicitor then went on to say: "By the way, she has also left all her money to you and your wife and there will be between £250,000 and £275,000 remaining, when all expenses have been sorted."

I declared the gift of £25,000 she had given us three years earlier, pointing it out in both hers and our bank statements. She had no one else to leave her money to: Jackie had passed away and she had no contact with her sister. The only way we knew about the estranged sister was when, four months before Joan died, a young man turned up with a framed photograph of the two sisters taken in Farnham. We thought it a little strange, but we put it up on her wall and then, when she passed, the son contacted the solicitors and asked for it back.

It struck me then that it was a good thing she had the common sense to have her solicitors as joint executors of her will, so that if anyone wanted to challenge it, they would have to go through them. I thought it was very smart of her, so much so that when I go, I will have the same arrangements with our eldest child, daughter Nicola, as the joint executor.

There was no challenge, and the death was advertised in the newspapers in case there was someone out there who felt they had a claim. There was no response and after a few months all was confirmed and a year later the money was transferred in segments to our account.

She died in June 2019 and Covid closed us all down in March 2020. By the time the solicitors had extracted their fees, there was still a quarter of a million pounds left, joining the other £25,000 she had gifted us in our bank account - and boy was that good timing!

The money was not wasted on a Bentley, a Rolls Royce or a cruise around the world. We thought we might buy a little place for ourselves in case we wanted to sell the hotel or simply move out, but the pandemic made the decision for us, and we used it to get us through the plague. We didn't have to borrow extra money from the government, as Mrs Profitt's bequest kept us and the hotel alive at a time when many were sinking.

I am sure she would have looked down on us and smiled that we had put her money to the best possible use, keeping alive the hotel she had fallen in love with.

We also did some refurbishments, concentrating on the restaurant, installing some wood panelling and a new floor, something if we had done during normal times, would have closed down our restaurant for six weeks or so.

Her money really kept us afloat during Covid. Without her gift we wouldn't have been able to upgrade the restaurant and we would probably have had to have a loan of £150,000 or more which, of course, would have had to been paid back with interest. Joan Proffitt was a genuine Fairy Godmother; a lovely, kind lady. So, if there is anyone out there who wants to leave their money to us, no problem, we will put it to good use! More seriously, she will be remembered and will be part of our hotel as long as we are there.

Do Not Disturb

There was another moment in time when I came within an ace of a large amount of cash that might have changed the course of our lives. I was still on the upwards ladder at the Grosvenor House Hotel when I was on one of our regular six-monthly clear out duties, going through the lost property left at out hotel. You would be surprised at what careless, forgetful guests can leave behind at their hotel lodgings. Six hundred pairs of ladies' knickers, 750 umbrellas, 40 cameras, all sorts of clothing, sex toys, crutches, even a prosthetic leg. Pornography used and discarded in all manner of hidey holes around the rooms, handbags, keys, belts, ties and, most frequent, spectacles, at least that was understandable! A lot went to charity but valuable items, such as jewellery and watches, could be claimed by the finder if all attempts to discover the owner had failed after six months of concerted efforts.

Apart from the lost property, there were also safe deposit boxes for guests to leave their property in the knowledge they would be coming back in a year or more to collect them on their next visit. There were probably two or three hundred of these locked metal boxes, stacked and recorded with numbers to match the keys. There were no spare keys and if the owner lost theirs, we would have to charge them to drill the lock out and replace it. But if a resident died and had not informed any of their surviving family of the existence of the security box, then it could remain unopened for eternity if we did not intervene. Those who lived in our apartments rarely had the foresight to mention their deposit boxes in their will for whatever reason.

When the reception area of Grosvenor House was refurbished five long forgotten safety boxes were unearthed. I checked with the security manager Steve, and he told me that some of them were recorded with the name of the key holder who we could try and contact. Many were out of date and untraceable and we called on maintenance to drill the locks. They did so and left them for Steve and I to have the excitement of looking through not one, but several Pandora's Boxes. There was jewellery of various values but nothing that exotic. There were documents, passports, a small amount of cash in a variety of currencies, a fancy watch or two, but nothing too exciting, as we came to the last box. Before we opened it Steve had a call to tell him there was a security alert but despite the disappointments, he was still keen to see what the final box held. I offered to look after it to let him go but he was as keen as me to see the contents. We opened it and…

BINGO!!!!!!

The box was crammed from top to bottom with bundles of British banknotes in cellophane packets. It was so full you would have struggled to slip another fifty pound note in with the rest. A quick count and we estimated we were talking about at least half a million pounds in unclaimed cash. We looked at each other and I am sure we had the same thought. Would anyone notice if we slipped a few of those packets in our pockets. Who would know? Had Steve been on his own maybe he would have been tempted. I know for sure that had I been on my own, I would have helped myself to at least £100,000 and he would probably have done the same. As it was, we turned it in and the hotel tried every way possible to trace an owner, even contacting the Saudi Arabian Embassy, who could not help. Loose change, I guess, to them. Sometime later it was realised that the same wealthy individual had also left behind a car, stored in our car park. When the covers were taken off it revealed a Ferrari. It was a veritable treasure trove, but Forte plc were the only benefactors. I have never forgotten and have never changed my mind. Had I been alone I would have filled my pockets….and my boots!

Tips, tronc, gratuities, handouts… or whatever you want to call them, are essential part of our industry but the laws governing them are now so complex you need a degree to discover what you can and what you cannot do with money gifted to the staff. When I was with Grosvenor House as a valet, we used to earn an absolute fortune from money given to us by the guests. There was no minimum wage just our salary, which was very low, and you relied on those tips, not just to supplement weekly wage, but to extend your earnings to sensible levels and put food on the table. It was very much like America is now, where staff at restaurants and hotels are totally reliant on the extras that are left on the table, added to the bill or pressed into expectant palms. Leave ten per cent over there and they will chase you down the road to demand more, leave nothing and they are just as likely to run down the road with a meat cleaver in hand to persuade you that something had been overlooked.

Personally, I am against service charges, especially when it spirals up and beyond twelve and a half percent. I don't agree with it at all, and I am of the belief that if the service has been good or better than expected, you leave a gratuity that reflects your satisfaction and pleasure, but if you feel it has been inferior you adjust and if it has been questionable, then leave nothing at all and tell them why. On a recent trip to Jersey everything we had on the hotel bill was subject to a service charge in excess of 10% and one of our meals in their restaurant for two came to over £300, when a service charge was added.

In my early days in London at the Grosvenor House Hotel, there was no service charge and in the Langham Hotel here in Eastbourne we still do not add a service charge. It is left totally to the discretion of the guest.

When I was a valet as a 15-year-old at the Grosvenor House, I also used to do overtime as a page boy and both jobs meant tips but, before that, as a washer upper, what we were paid was what we got, and it wasn't much. We didn't have to share the gratuities, you kept what you were given but I had an arrangement with my colleague who shared the duties over two floors, that we would also share the tips. That was our own personal arrangement, and the management did not interfere.

The head doorman would also have his own understanding and when he was slipped a fiver by the incoming guest, he would get the porter to take the bags away and give him a pound out of his tip. It was much the same for the concierge, then called the hall porter, who earned his golden cross keys on his lapel (look out for them, they still wear them). They have their own worldwide society and are amongst the highest paid people in the hospitality industry simply because of gratuities. When I was working as a valet, I personally used to pay £8 a year to the taxman in lieu of my extras, even though I was probably getting around a thousand pounds a year. It was all legitimate and accepted by the hotel and HMRC.

When I assumed control at the Langham, I inherited the tip system which meant that any cash left in the bedrooms for the chambermaids, in the restaurant, the bar or reception, would all go into the tronc, a central pot, and was shared out with all of the staff at the end of the month. We continued with it, based on hours worked. It was shared out according to your hours so, obviously, someone who worked 40 hours would get four times as much as someone who had only done ten. I thought this was fair enough and didn't interfere. Everybody was included from the washer up, who has no contact with the guests at all, through to the receptionists, who deals with them and their problems all the time. Neither Wendy nor I as management and owners, took anything out of the tronc. When we debated it with the staff and asked them if they wanted to carry on with the old system, the answer was a unanimous yes. The money was shared out, put in brown envelopes and given to the staff member at the end of the month, all overseen by Wendy. It was all tax free – or so we thought…

I should have been more thorough as an experienced hotelier, and it caught up with me when Her Majesty's finest investigated. I received a letter from the tax office, having been chosen at random, which I passed on to my accountant. I wasn't bothered because neither my wife nor I, despite working up to 90 hours a week and always being on duty round the clock, took anything from the pot. I have had my share of tips over the years and as far as I was concerned it was the staff's money and helped keep them happy and content. One of the questions my accountants asked was what I did with the tronc box, and I told him. He held up his hands in horror and told me we couldn't do that because the tax man wanted his 20 per cent cut. The law had passed me by, and I told him that, instead of a tronc, we would let the staff keep their own tips. But again, the idea was met with a firm shake of the head, warning me that they might well come down and do a spot check. I thought there was little chance of that unless they happened to be in Eastbourne on holiday. But he pointed out that once they had their teeth into you, they could go back five, six, seven years and he persuaded me to write a letter, owning up and the reasons why, sign it and he would deal with the response from the tax office.

He eventually came back and told me he had spoken personally to the inspector, and he had agreed that I hadn't been trying to fiddle them and clearly, I had made nothing out of what was a genuine mistake. Instead of taking my punishment back many years as they could have done, they decided to tax me for 18 months and suddenly I found myself paying a bill of £15,000, despite neither of us having taken a penny in tips. It was a lesson learned: an experienced hotelier of many years, I had got it wrong and had to pay the price. I was disappointed, but in myself, not anyone else. I should have been aware and known better. I paid it off with ill grace, at the same time appreciating it could have been a lot more.

Clearly our system had to change, something I had to explain to the staff. The rules were that we had to have two tronc masters, nominated by the staff and not by us. The staff had a vote and decided on Sue, the head housekeeper, along with the head receptionist. The pair had to count the cash together that had been given. We also had to give the tax office their names, positions in the company and their home addresses. From that moment on, the tips from all round the hotel had to be put in a tin which is kept behind reception, whether they were from the housekeeper, the restaurant manager or the bar.

On a couple of occasions, it was discovered that tips had NOT been passed on, but trousered by a couple of the staff. You can imagine that didn't go down well with their colleagues and they were blackballed by the rest of the staff and did not hang around for too long afterwards before quitting.

I discovered the miscreants in the Langham quite easily. Guests would come up to me as the owner and tell me how well (or badly) they had been looked after by certain members of staff. Often they revealed they had given the good ones a tip as a thank you and it was a simple step from there to reception to check who had put money in the tin. When it failed to happen the first time, I approached the member of staff concerned, told him effusively of how pleased the customers had been with the food and the service ... and then asked him what had happened to the fiver tip they told me they had given him. The transaction would be denied but I would then pass on the information to another member of staff and within the hour everyone knew that they had been robbed of a share of a fiver. They were then blackballed, not with black or white balls, but by not speaking to the culprit. Sent to Coventry and within a week they were gone.

But there was no need for black balls with the Inland Revenue. Their word was law and if you stepped the wrong side of the line, they had you. In this instance it was all sorted out and they let us pay our fine over the course of the year so that it didn't hit too hard.

Our staff realised we had inadvertently stepped outside the law, and they were only too happy to accept the new regime with all tips now handed over to two appointed cashiers. The two Tronc Masters, as they were called, would then take the counted money to Wendy and say, "Here's four grand for the Tronc." It then had to be counted again and put in our bank, under a separate account labelled gratuity, every month. It was divided by the hours worked and paid off with the wages with the correct money going directly to the taxman. It was all done by computer and all above board.

So now, good customer, you know that for every fiver you leave in the room for the staff, the taxman immediately claims their share before it is passed on to the people it was meant for. It came about because several very famous chefs got caught pocketing a large portion of the tips the customers had left for the staff. They were taking up to eight per cent for themselves before a law was brought in which clipped their wings considerably. I thought it was disgusting that these leading lights of our industry, many of whom were supplementing their considerable incomes with television shows and books, were, to my mind, stealing from their staff, many of whom were being paid the minimum wage. If celebrity chefs are turning over £5 million a year, then eight per cent plus is an awful lot of someone else's cash. They were all fined and thoroughly deserved it, with no sympathy from me.

Do Not Disturb

The tax man also did the doormen from the big London hotels one year, demanding to see bank balances and then going through them with a fine toothcomb with both parties knowing full well what was going on. The taxman will always win, especially once it is evident that someone is making large purchases and cannot back it up with their salary. Once they have their hooks into you, watch out. We might not always like paying so much to the taxman but that is what funds the running of the country.

My philosophy is very simple. It would be easy to bang the table and say I am not paying the added charge after an unsatisfactory meal, but I am a hotelier and don't want to make a scene and spoil other customers' night out. I simply never return to that restaurant and if I am asked for an opinion of the hotel or restaurant in question, I will give an honest answer. I have the same attitude for cruises, where I would much prefer to sit on a table for two with my wife and make my own judgement on the quality of the service, rather than sit with people I don't know and boast about who I am and what I have done. When I am asked what I do for a living I tell them, truthfully, I am a washer upper. Some don't talk to you again. They are snobs and it suits me not to have to mix with them.

Although I no longer benefit, I admit I am the best detective in the world when it comes to sniffing out the person who dares take money from the pockets of his friends and co-workers and I won't hesitate in letting their colleagues know. I warn them when they come on board at my hotel and they know the consequences, backed up by the stories relayed to them by their new workmates. It still happens. But not often. I know the damage it can cause and when I was in London, I even saw arguments over tips break out into fights. A ten shilling note was a lot of money in those days when you were only earning twelve quid a week.

I have a friend who works in a smart London eatery, and he regularly takes home £800 a month in tips, tax paid, which gives him a very comfortable way of living. So, tips, whether it is a pound coin left on the bar or £25,000 handed over in £20 notes by some rich sheik, it keeps the wheels oiled in the huge business of hospitality. Without them it would all grind to a halt.

CHAPTER FIVE

DO NOT DISTURB

The old saying goes that you can choose your friends but not your relatives. With the hotel trade there is another dimension altogether. The hotel guests. Some are an absolute delight and, indeed, over the years many have become friends, but others not so, and you never know what lies beyond the bedroom door with the ubiquitous "Do Not Disturb" notice hanging from the doorknob. It doesn't matter what sort of hotel it is, five-star London with all the bells and whistles, or our four-rosette rated seaside resort in Eastbourne.

Don't ask the general manager or the owner, just ask the poor chambermaids who must cross their fingers and everything else when they come across the sign that could mean anything from a couple of old age pensioners having a well-earned lie in after walking the South Downs or Mr and Mrs Smith – a typical nom de plume used by adulterous couples wanting to cover their tracks – enjoying a noisy, illicit weekend, with a rarely used view of the sea lapping the shore outside their ceiling to floor windows.

A chambermaid at the Langham Hotel was certainly unsure when she saw a hooded person come out of room 115, a smaller single room. She checked her list, and her memory served her well, the room should have been empty, it was officially empty and unsold. In fact, it was one she was due to deep clean. This was early January, and the hotel was not full, so who the hell was that going to down the stairs and why was there a "Do Not Disturb" notice hanging on the knob? We were all baffled, the bed had been used along with the towels, but there was nothing to suggest who had used it. We decided to keep an eye open the next day to see if we could solve the mystery. She assured us that the room had been cleaned the day before and was due that deep clean before the next guest checked in.

Sure, enough the next morning the chambermaid, on the look-out after her experience 24 hours earlier, spotted the hooded stranger emerge again from the single room.

"Hello, hello," she called out, hurrying to catch up with the unknown guest, only to find her progress halted abruptly by a sharp slap across the face. That was enough and she promptly sought out her boss who came to me in the office and explained what had happened. She quickly explained that the person heading out of the hotel's front door had just emerged from a room which should have been empty and that the staff member had been attacked when she tried to stop them.

That was enough for me, and I leapt up and saw this hooded person hurrying through our main doors.

"Is that the person?" I asked and getting the nod I sprinted out and down the steps just as the uninvited visitor turned left into Royal Parade. I grabbed at their shoulder and as I swung the interloper around, I took a hefty slap across the face.

The son of a boxer of some stature and a bit of a boxer myself before running took over my sporting life, I reacted as any red-blooded South London boy would have done and unleashed a tasty little right hook right on the point of the jaw and down the stranger went.

It was only then that I realised to my horror that I had laid out a woman and no matter how much she deserved it, it was not something I would knowingly do in any circumstances. Almost at the very moment she hit the ground and the hood slipped, a car pulled up and a voice shouted, "Stay where you are, you're nicked!" It was a guy in casual clothes, driving an unmarked car.

Odder and odder. "What do you mean, I'm nicked," I asked, "Who are you?"

He told me he was an off-duty policeman who had witnessed what had happened and as he came over to nick her, the girl bounced up and began screaming and shouting that I had punched her, and that it was me who should be arrested.

Nice turn of events, I thought as I tried to explain to the plain clothes

Do Not Disturb

man that I owned the hotel and she had assaulted both me and one of my staff and had been caught coming out of a room that she had not paid for.

She was still fighting like a hell cat, and the officer told me to go inside while he was on his phone calling the station for back up. The witch spotted some wooden planks from a refurbishment waiting to be collected, picked one up one, complete with nails, and began hammering it against the glass doorway which I stood behind, waiting for developments.

This was my property she was damaging, and I stepped out to stop her, grabbing the timber so that she could not hit me and called out to the copper to get his backside over and arrest this woman before she did serious damage to me or my property.

At last, my demands prompted action. He terminated his call, raced over and handcuffed the wild woman to stop her hurting me, him or herself, and hustled her into the backseat of his car. Back up soon arrived and she was taken away cursing and screaming, while I was ushered back into the hotel to be questioned.

I was more bothered at how this girl had got into my hotel and into one of my bedrooms for two successive nights. It transpired she had climbed some scaffolding at the back of the hotel and, out of sight, found a window that was unlocked and let herself in. She made herself comfortable, drank the tea and hot chocolate, ate the complimentary biscuits, and then let herself out of the front door the next day before returning the same way to spend a second night.

Eventually the local police came back and told me they were not going to arrest me for grievous bodily harm as she had struck me first and that when they searched her at the station, they found the key to Room 115 in her pocket! Perhaps she planned to move in permanently, who knows? It seems she had come down during the night and with the night porter off doing his usual chores, she took the opportunity to pop the key to "her" room into her pocket. But they also quickly discovered that she had a rap sheet as long as the piece of wood she attacked me with. A thief, a druggie and a ne'er do well.

The police asked me if I wanted to press charges, but I declined, told them to leave it but just to warn her never to come near my hotel again. I didn't ask her name and thankfully never saw her again. It was a great punch, wasted.

She asked the police to apologise to me because I refused to see her, which I accepted and left it at that. I was more concerned for my chambermaid who had been assaulted, but she didn't want her day in court either.

It was also a far better result than a previous incident in my first job in an hotel, the magnificent Grosvenor House in opulent Park Lane, when I thought I had murdered a guest.

I worked in the elite hotel for 28 years, going from washing up the dirty pots and pans to the general manager's job,

When the incident occurred, I was still easing my way up the ladder and held the title of assistant duty manager, quite an important job because you get lumbered with everything from the chef cutting his finger while slicing the vegetables to complaints from guests that their steak wasn't cooked to instructions, or their room has the wrong view. All the sorts of grievances that were deemed to be below general manager level but well within the compass of his assistant.

On this occasion housekeeping called me through the switchboard to tell me that the couple in Apartment Four hadn't been seen since Friday and as it was now Monday, they were becoming concerned. There was a "Do Not Disturb" notice on the door and they had been unable to raise them on the house telephone, so would the duty manager – me – sort it out.

The staff had previously tried to open the door, but it would only shift a couple of inches due to something blocking the way, and they were not able to look into the room to see if all was well with the occupants.

The first thing I did was to call security as back up. It was never wise to go into unknown situations without someone who could substantiate your story should things go awry. You are taught that in your training so that you always had a witness and not get lumbered with the old "he said, she said" situation.

We met outside Apartment 4 where the couple had been living for eight months. Grosvenor House had 160 private apartments in one block and 452 bedrooms in the other. These clients were well to do Americans, in their late forties, very respectable, quiet and good patrons. Naturally I tried the phone first, no answer, knocked on their door, no answer, and I eventually used my master key to open the door. Sure, enough it opened just a sliver and no further, no matter how much I pushed and shoved. It was a two-bedroom apartment, separate lounge, large en-suite bathroom and totally in the dark with the light switch just out of my reach.

No matter how hard I pushed I couldn't shift the door. I could clearly hear it striking something solid but, whatever it was, a chair or a suitcase, I was unable to budge it no matter how hard I shoved, not even when I put my shoulder against it and used all my strength.

I eventually managed to increase the gap to four or so inches, just enough to reach my hand in and switch on the lights. To my horror the obstruction was neither a suitcase nor a chair, but the head of the male guest with his torso stretched out behind him so that he could not easily be moved by pushing to door.

All my heaving and shoving had done serious damage to the man's face. One eye was hanging out, his face smashed in, with cuts and indentations and the bodily fluids spilling out and staining the cream carpet. I told the security man, a former policeman, to come and have a look, as I didn't know whether he was alive or dead, although I had a pretty good idea from just looking at him that he wouldn't be down for breakfast.

The police and ambulance arrived within minutes of the emergency call and I was later assured that the man had been dead for at least 14 hours. I was relieved to know I hadn't killed him but I still have nightmares from time to time about that day. I consider myself a tough enough guy, but I still recall the moment I switched on the light and looked down to see the face that I had bashed in. I still get upset when I think about it.

CHAPTER SIX

THE GOOD, BAD AND THE COVID

Hotels suffer more than most when there is any sort of crisis, national or international. At any given moment the rug can be pulled from under you with recessions, terrorism, deaths, industrial upheaval, fires, floods, power failures, all testing the will of the hotel and its senior staff.

Whatever happens you can be almost certain that you are not the first to have to deal with it and help is usually at hand from the necessary sources, the government, the police, the fire brigade, the ambulance services and, quite often, good Samaritans.

Then there was Covid, the pandemic which came in, so they say, from a laboratory in China and closed not only hotels of every shape and size, but pretty well everything else.

Even this wasn't entirely new as, in 1346, the world was struck down by the Black Death, a combination of Bubonic and Pneumonic plagues, which began, ironically, they say, in China, and swept through the world, carried from country to country and continent to continent by trade ships. Estimates of between 25 million and 50 million perished, but no one really knew or could count the cost around the world in the seven years it spread.

It couldn't happen again they said – but it did, and although far fewer died as a result the estimate is still a scary seven million and once again figures are likely to have been fudged. The consequences for everyone were devastating and none more so than the leisure and hospitality industry which was shut down almost overnight when the pandemic struck the United Kingdom in March 2020.

No one, not the government, the boffins, the health authorities, had a clue what to do because there were no modern precedents, nothing to guide them.

So, they closed everything and told people to stay indoors and when they had to go out it was for an hour only and then to keep at least two metres away from the nearest person.

Pubs, clubs, restaurants, coffee bars and hotels, were shut down until further notice. The government did their best, helping where they could but no one could do the right thing because no one knew what the right thing was.

The government closed the Langham Hotel, as they did everyone else, and we had around 50 staff who had to be told we were shutting down until who knew when and that they were not to come into work from that moment on and until further notice, while some on casual contracts simply had to go completely. We could offer them nothing.

Like everyone else, we didn't know what was going on, how long it would last and where it left us. Naturally we were grateful for the help from the government with assistance for some of the wage bill, but we hadn't a clue what the future held.

I met each and every one of my staff personally, 55 of them, helped by my wife Wendy and our General Manager Simon Brown. The majority I told we would keep them informed of what was going on when we knew, while others I had to apologize to and simply let go. I told them honestly that I couldn't afford to retain all of them, and I chopped my staff by about twenty.

Wendy and I were left in our living quarters in the Langham Hotel on our own, a strange situation as in the hotel next door they were taking people in off the streets. I have nothing but sympathy for the genuine homeless, but these were drifters and wasters and some of them misbehaved badly, knowing there was little or no visible law enforcement to watch them.

Gangs of them would go down to the Salvation Army headquarters to pick up free food, then back to the Strand Hotel where they had been housed. When they had eaten their fill, they threw the packaging and uneaten food over my wall or in the road in front of my hotel, which I had to clean up personally. I tried to talk to them but just got back a mouthful of abuse and threats of physical harm. I suppose it was around 10% of them who were the problem and most of that group, it seemed to me, were on drugs.

For much of the homeless and refugees from Eastern Europe, I felt sorry but not for those who threw the food away and treated me and my wife disrespectfully. The government did the right thing taking them off the streets but there wasn't the manpower nor willpower to supervise them.

Wendy and I sat in reception manning the phone with booked guests calling to ask for their money back or to ask what the future arrangements were. Most were really nice, especially our regulars, many of whom just said to keep the deposit and they would use it when the pandemic was over, and they were able to return.

Those who wanted their money back, we repaid within ten days or so but at least we were around, and they had someone to talk to and sort out the finances one way or the other. That was something that was not happening everywhere, as hotel doors were locked and bolted with no one to man the switchboard or anything else.

We took the opportunity of having a completely empty restaurant to carry out some refurbishment we had been planning before Covid struck. We decided to go ahead with wood panelling the restaurant to dado height as we had already purchased some of the materials. We managed to get a carpenter friend to come in and carry out the work, although it wasn't easy to buy the extra wood we needed to finish the job, as builders merchants were closed and everything had to be ordered online and collected by ourselves in our car. However, we managed to finish the job in the first lockdown with a local painter coming in to spray paint the wood panelling in a colour to offset the William Morris wallpaper we had selected for parts of the restaurant, including the now popular 'blue alcove'.

After reopening in August 2020, the hotel was busy in spite of the restrictions which meant we had to install screens in front of the reception desk and bar, no cash sales were allowed and customers and staff had to wear the dreaded face masks in all public areas. No one could travel abroad so hotels in the UK were fully booked with people wanting to get away after months of being stuck at home.

The government decided it would be helpful for hospitality businesses who had suffered badly during lockdown to introduce a new scheme 'Eat Out to Help Out' where we offered customers a 50% discount on all food and non-alcoholic drinks and were reimbursed by the government. That summer turned out to be a scorcher and we were inundated! As soon as a table was vacated in the bar or on the terrace it was full again with happy punters delighted to be out again and making the most of the 50% discount. It was hard work and our restaurant and bar staff were very pleased when the scheme was discontinued at the end of August!

We were then struck with the second lockdown just before Christmas 2020 meaning all our planned festivities had to be cancelled. We took advantage of this second period of closure to install a new cocktail bar in one of the restaurant alcoves. Once again our carpenter friend was able to oversee the construction and it was finished in time for reopening in January.

We asked the local artist who had designed and made all our stunning stained glass windows to come up with designs for the two windows in the cocktail bar area and we were delighted with the results. Now all the original plain glass windows in the restaurant have been replaced with images of Eastbourne landmarks, the lighthouse at Beachy Head, the Long Man of Wilmington, Eastbourne Pier, Seven Sisters, etc. We also have a stained glass window in the Bar depicting the RNLI lifeboat in action with a collection box for donations.

Back to Covid, and just as we thought we could reopen in January, the third lockdown was announced and we were closed again right through until the middle of May! Once again we took the opportunity to do some more work on the restaurant, this time taking up the old worn carpet and replacing it with parquet effect tiles. We were planning to take out the old ceiling tiles and raise the ceiling as we had done in the reception area and bar but luckily no more lockdowns so we haven't got round to that yet!

Even when we were back in business there was still a hangover, with staff calling in sick far more often than in pre Covid days and even more serious for restaurants and hotels all over the world, was the difficulty in getting old staff back or new people to replace them. So many had moved on to other things in life, indeed, many even moving home to a different part of the country or abroad.

Lots found it easier to work shifts at their local supermarket than work unsociable hours for more or less the same money they would earn in an hotel. When we resumed operations, we were ten staff short, a lot for an hotel of our size.

It took us a while to get back up to strength. We had lost staff in the areas where shifts were necessary, such as the chefs with breakfast, lunch, and dinner to cater for. They would come to work in the morning starting work at 5.30am and if they didn't do breakfast, they would do lunch and afternoon tea, go home and then back at 5.30pm to cook dinner, probably not returning home until around midnight.

The consequences were clear, relationships broke down, marriages ended in divorce. Chefs were the most vulnerable as they were ones who did the most splits shifts and second were the restaurant staff followed by the kitchen porters. Not so much a problem if you are a big five star hotel and you can afford to have double the staff with a kitchen porter doing a shift and then a second coming in for the late shift, but it was not something we or others of our level could afford.

Covid made us more than ever aware of the dramatic effects an economic crisis could have on us. I went through a couple of recessions while I was working in London, particularly during the Gulf war when people weren't travelling to hotels; the Americans stopped coming over and foreign holidays were limited. We had to make 500 staff redundant out of 2,000, taking six months to shed them as gently as we could. Terribly sad because they had done nothing wrong, but there were not sufficient customers to go round.

It was the same with Covid. We could cope at first when we returned to work on a limited basis, especially when the rate of VAT was reduced. We were busy and we were making money. Everyone rallied round to keep the business going, with Wendy and I doing even more hours, serving in the restaurant, in the bar, working in the kitchen. I continued to be mine host as well while Wendy worked reception, did the accounts, housekeeping, and anything else that fell in her path.

The staff could see we were backing them up and they were appreciative seeing the bosses working even harder than they were. We were always prepared to get our hands dirty, and it was acknowledged.

We also looked after them and if they worked seven -hours and five minutes they were paid for seven hours and fifteen minutes, we never took it to the nearest hour in our favour. It wasn't a time to be mean or unfair.

Perhaps more hotels, restaurants and clubs would have survived but for the follow up when Russia invaded Ukraine and caused a global energy crisis, with prices skyrocketing.

The result for us hoteliers was carnage as the price of gas and electricity increased exponentially, throwing our carefully worked out schedules and profit margins out of the window and as the bills came in, followed by the VAT and other tax charges, so the leisure industry began to shrink again with no breathing space after the dreaded Covid.

It has changed everything and little in the leisure industry will be the same again.

CHAPTER SEVEN

THE CUSTOMER IS NOT ALWAYS RIGHT

One of the most repeated sayings in the customer related services is the old chestnut that the customer is always right. Not on your nelly. You may have to leave them thinking their complaint has substance and while you always have to investigate, quite often the customer is hopelessly wrong! I won't tell them to their face, but I will in print.

I was reminded of this fact as I was preparing to add to my manuscript when the receptionist warned me in the Langham Hotel that one of a female clients had a bit of a face on her, in fact she was quite grumpy. She had asked for two coffees, one a decaffeinated and the other a flat latte. They were served to her and her friend on the terrace with its glorious view of the sea from Royal Parade, when she came back into reception to complain that she didn't get her café latte as requested.

The receptionist knew this not to be true as he had checked it himself and when she said it wasn't satisfactory, because it was not strong enough, he offered to inject more coffee. She went off muttering that it was not good enough and stopping long enough to ask a member of staff if the prices had gone up as well.

They had, of course, as they had everywhere, since Covid. I went out to do my duty as owner, taking my time, talking to other customers on the way. This is something I feel is crucial in our business to have face to face contact, it costs nothing and if the customers have a problem, they share it with me because they know I am Neil, the owner. I eventually made my way to the two women, said my hellos, and asked why she was grumpy as I knew that would wind her up. She explained they had ordered her coffee, didn't get it and when she did, it wasn't very strong. I thought from her name she had been with us before, although I didn't recognise her and asked if she had ordered the same drink previously. She said she had and had been happy. I pointed out that every cup was Colombian ground coffee, measured in a bag which was then opened and poured into the cup. My man had put in three, just to make sure but she responded that she had been in the week before when the coffee was fine. Finessing her complaint, she added that the waiter who served her was a bit off and this time her friend backed her up. Rather than apologise for something I had not personally witnessed or heard about, I went and checked with the waiter who pointed out that only one of the ladies came in to place the order and that she herself was a bit offish with him.

When I put it to the ladies that only one had spoken to the waiter the argument was over. I wanted the truth and not some made up story which could have got one of my staff into trouble for nothing.

That is my philosophy, and I would rather lose a lying customer, complaining simply for complaining's sake or to show off, than lose a good member of staff. She was a miserable grumpy, old thing who was having a bad day. She was right about the prices having gone up marginally but, as I told her, she could have mentioned it the previous week when she came in when the prices had just increased.

I will always apologise if something is genuinely wrong, and I will take steps to improve it. That was something I had to do more regularly when I worked for someone else in someone else's hotel, but this was MY hotel, and I can say exactly what I like and if they don't like it, they can go and be miserable somewhere else.

On another occasion I was on duty at the Langham reception desk when a man arrived to check in with his mate. They went upstairs and one came back down straight away and was being rude to one of the female staff, bringing her to the verge of tears. I intervened and asked him what was wrong, and he said he wanted a sea view. I tried to explain that when he arrived all the sea views had been allocated and he was given and charged for what he had booked. I checked and found we did have a sea view because of a non-arrival, and I told him myself, but instead of a smile and a thank you he refused to pay the additional £25 and demanded to know who I was. I said to him I was the owner and asked what his name was. I told him it was very simple;

you wanted a sea view and I have found you one and you have to pay the going rate the same as anyone else.

He was adamant. He wanted a sea view but wasn't going to pay any extra for it. He compounded his felony by asking who the silly cow was on the desk. I wouldn't have liked that sort of comment whoever it was, but it happened to be Wendy, my wife. I had now had enough of him and his attitude. He was blustering, rude and using the sort of language we don't encourage, so I gave him his original key back, told him to go back to his room, get his bags and his friend, and to bugger off and not come back. He came back still angry, forcing his face and body close to mine, I tossed the cup of tea I was drinking straight in his face.

My hotel, my rules and I didn't want him in what is also my home insulting my wife and pushing his face aggressively into mine. When he came back down, he walked off with my key and wouldn't return it. It was like two kids in the playground, I took his bag and said he could have it when he returned my key and if he refused, I would bring in the police. He was now past apologising, even though he had been given his deposit back, so I did what I promised and called in the local constabulary. He sat outside and I waited with his bag inside before a patrol car drove past an hour later. He suddenly leapt to his feet and ran straight into the road in front of the car. The policewoman jumped out and went mad at him for almost causing an accident. She wasn't even responding to my call but another one. After phoning in to the station to tell them she had been detained from the original call, she asked what was going on, I explained who I was and what had happened. He retorted by telling her that I had thrown tea in his face, and he wanted to charge me with assault.

I was marched back into my hotel, and she interviewed me privately while her colleague talked to him. She returned my key, and I gave her his suitcase. She warned me that I may hear more if he pressed charges which he promptly did. I got myself together, got in my car and followed her to the station where I was interviewed, prints taken, photographed and a swab was taken from my mouth, before being shown into a cell where I sat on the bed wondering what next.

Suddenly a loud voice in my ear made me leap a foot in the air before I realised it was an intercom and they were only asking me if I wanted a cup of tea. At that stage I could have done with something stronger. I sat there for a second hour before someone eventually came and told me I could go and that there were not going to be any charges.

They had also taken the trouble of speaking to the receptionist, not my wife, who confirmed he had been rude and insulting to her and confirmed that I had responded to him and told him to leave. The odd thing was that his mate was on the periphery and the only time he spoke was to tell his friend not to be so stupid and to leave quietly. That was it. I never heard or saw either of them again and I left Eastbourne police nick a free man, leaving behind the swab, the prints, my photograph and my statement.

People can be rude and obnoxious and that is why I say that the customer is not always right. I came from a different era and after spending 38 years working for other people, I now owned my own hotel and after 20 years of being my own boss I reserve the right to tell someone I don't like them, and they could not to stay in my hotel.

I guess in my years in Eastbourne I have ejected around twenty people, sounds a lot but it is only around one a year. Much of it is caused by drink.

More recently I was sitting in my office doing the paperwork while Wendy was in reception on a late shift covering for a member of staff who was on holiday. I was just coming out of my office before her shift ended at around 9.30pm, when a security man would take over. The door automatically locks at night with the guests able to gain entry by using their key card. We back this up with a *Residents Only* sign to stop strange people, druggies, drunks and strays wandering in off the street. Wendy told me that there was a man outside shouting through the door. I called over the assistant manager, Miguel, to join me so that I had a witness and asked him the man what he wanted. He let loose a volley of four letter words, said he was staying at the hotel and wanted to be let in. I asked him for his name, and he said that Miguel knew who he was, a statement immediately rebuffed. It was clear where this was going but I played it out, asking him for his room number. The number he gave did not exist, so I opened the door and told him to clear off. He wouldn't let it go and I became really angry and pushed him over when he encroached on my space. We had called the police by this time and when he ran off, he was intercepted by the two patrol cars. When they stopped him, he accused me of hitting him without cause. The policeman knew who I was but still had to investigate. I explained how it had evolved and how he was rude to my wife and myself, using profane and threatening language and that I hadn't hit him, just thrown him to the ground as the CCTV cameras would clearly show. I told him he was upsetting my customers. The officer then revealed this yobo was already on parole for beating up his girlfriend. There were witnesses to back up my story and he was led away and this time I stayed clear of the cells.

It is not just men. I have also had problems with girls. One incident occurred a few weeks after having a hip replacement operation. We had a big tribute evening, an ABBA night, in our restaurant with the usual full house. It was around March, and I had managed to get rid of one of my crutches after my operation but was still reliant on the other one. Sleep remained a problem and after the show, I was restless and around 2am, I got up to go to the loo in my apartment. I heard noises outside, looked out of my window and saw two girls walking past the hotel, very drunk, cursing and blinding and holding each other up. I prayed they weren't staying with us but, sure enough, they stumbled up the stairs to the front door. I muttered a few curses myself and naked but for the dressing gown and hobbling on one crutch, I went to see what was happening. My staff are well trained and although the security man was new, having been with us just six or seven weeks, at that time of night, he knew he was not to let them in. But when they claimed they were staying with us and offered him a legitimate room number, he let them in. I went into reception to be met by a volley of abuse, the least of which was being called an old paedophile. By this time the new boy realised he had dropped a clanger and when I asked the girls if they were staying with us, I was met with another barrage of abusive four letter words. I didn't take offence and told them they were very drunk, not staying at my hotel and to leave forthwith. They had take-away food in their hands and dribbling out of their mouths onto my carpet. I nearly had them out of the front door, when one of them said we are not going anywhere and stuck two fingers up at me. That was enough for me, I threw down my stick and went to eject them, but it was too soon after my operation and I was struggling with the new lad looking on open mouthed and doing nothing.

One of the girls smashed her mobile phone into my face, cutting me above the eye and although I would never deliberately hit a woman, I launched myself at them, gave her a right hander and she went straight on the floor. I told the lad to call the police, who arrived in two cars within minutes. I told them who I was and what had happened as I looked round for my crutch and tried to protect my modesty with my dressing gown. They took me into the bar to question me and the girls were questioned in reception.

There was suddenly a huge kerfuffle from reception where the girls had started fighting and swearing at the police. I rest my case m'lord. They were marched off and I told the officer, who was questioning me, that I had given one of them a slap in self-defence. They asked me if I wanted to press charges and I declined but the policewoman they attacked charged them with GBH.

Some of my staff and I later watched the scene played back on our CCTV and they all complimented me on a great right hander!

The customer is always right. Don't make me laugh. Were they right? They weren't even staying with us, but lied and said they were. There was a sad consequence, however, as a week later I had to let the security man go because he hadn't followed instructions and had not done his job correctly despite being fully trained. There were 90 people staying that night and he put everyone at risk by allowing two drunks in before first checking that their claims they were staying were true. One quick check of the register would have confirmed they were lying, and the door never needed to be opened.

Do Not Disturb

Just after Covid I was delighted and thrilled that so many customers were returning, some just to show their support for me and the hotel. We opened, still had the rules over masks with gel dispensers everywhere, struggling for staff and wondering what the future held for my large investment. One evening I was helping out in the kitchen where we were short staffed when I heard a lot of noise coming from the restaurant where we had 30 or 40 customers. It was emanating from a young lady who I went over to speak to. She and her male friend had got through two bottles of wine at the table, and I told her quietly that she would not be served with any more drink. With that the man got up and went to his room and, so I discovered later, picked up his bag and checked out, apparently embarrassed at the fuss she was causing.

He apologised to the receptionist on the way out and asked her to pass on his apologies to me. I did not know any of this was going on but to cut down the irritation to our other customers, I told her there was a telephone call for her and I would take her out to show her where she could take it. She stood up unsteadily and held onto my arm as I showed her out of the room. When we went through the door, I admitted to her that there was no call and that she had to calm down, be quiet and not upset other people who were trying to enjoy their dinner. I told her that she would have to leave, and I went up to her room with her and discovered she had not even unpacked, which at least made it easier for me. I was not surprised to find a half bottle of vodka empty in the bin and another in a drawer. I could also see that her partner had taken his case and left. When I returned, she said she had cancer, but I told her she was rude, obnoxious and that I didn't want her in my hotel. She immediately blew off again going through her repertoire of curses while I called for a taxi to take her away, put her bag in the car and told her to find another hotel.

I had to go back into the restaurant and apologise to all my customers table by table. She telephoned the next day to apologise and asked if she could come back. I told her I didn't want her in my building ever again. This was a nasty piece of work and further proof that the customer is not always right.

It was a different level at the Grosvenor House where riches or fame sometimes seems to entitle people. But they were even more obnoxious because they had money and therefore, thought they could do what they liked. It was not so much the regular clientele, apart from the odd eccentric who stayed with us, but more those who attended the functions. Every night we would end up with 1200-1300 people in a room which could hold 2,000, as large a room as you could find in an hotel anywhere in Europe. As ever it was alcohol at the root cause of the problems with many drinking and few footing the bill, often paid for by some company. They were largely attended by men with many of them consuming far too much because it was free, falling about, being rude and arrogant to the staff and exposing the real side of their character with barrack room language. Most of the year they are ordinary average workers and suddenly on one night they live like lords and think they own the world. As the night wears on so their behaviour slides and once the bosses have either gone home or scuttled off to their rooms, it really takes off. That's when they stick it on the bill and get really paralytic.

The wine waiters who were only too happy to serve them, would often scoop up the half empty and sometimes completely full bottles of wine at the end of the night, not to mention the bottles of spirits which had been ordered, signed for and left. These were casual staff brought in from an agency and they would even sell the same bottle back to the customer on a nearby table. It was a racket, but we caught them in the end and fired about twenty of them. We went through their staff lockers and found dozens of bottles of booze.

The customer is always right…….. except when they are wrong.

CHAPTER EIGHT

THE LONG AND WINDING ROAD

The journey from the kitchen to, in 1993, the office and the title of general manager of the Grosvenor House Hotel had taken 28 years and I could be forgiven for feeling a little smug and self-satisfied. After all it had been my target for a long while and although I was only caretaker in the senior role, I felt it was a formality that it would soon be made permanent. I had more experience in working in more departments than any previous general manager, I loved the job and it showed. I learned a great deal from the Forte family on how to run a business and, in particular, hotels, and had got to know Sir Rocco Forte in the late-seventies and later when we ran eight marathons together, seven in London and one in New York.

But my castle was built on quicksand as Rocco revealed when, out of the blue, he invited me to go on a run with him, something we had not done together for a while. It transpired it was rather like me taking one of my staff for a walk around the car park before sacking them, for early on in the run he told me what a great job I had done for the hotel, but they were going to move me on.

Tail between my legs I returned, temporarily, to being caretaker general manager. Rocco softened it as much as he was able, telling me that he had asked the area director to give me the general manager's job at the Berystede Hotel in Ascot, with the idea that I should go there for a couple of years to gain experience as a general manager and then return to London in a leading role at one of their five star hotels, possibly the Waldorf.

Neil Kirby

Neil running with Sir Rocco Forte in London Marathon 1982 raising £50,000 for the Hotel and Catering Trades Benevolent Fund.

Rocco explained that he had a particular interest in the Berystede which had 91 bedrooms, and that he was personally embarrassed about it as it was a short distance away from both Sunningdale and Wentworth Golf clubs and he was getting a number of complaints about the place. He wanted me to take it up to an AA four star hotel and then dangled the carrot of the Waldorf in front of me. Nothing so simple. He had not taken into account what others might feel about the arbitrary appointment. The current manager at the Berystede was still in situ and no one had told him he was about to be replaced and an unholy row erupted with me at the epicentre.

Their solution was to send me to the King Edward Hotel in Toronto for a couple of weeks to study the food and beverage side of the operation, an area where I admit I did not have the expertise, but to fly me all the way to Canada was a stretch. I was sure I was being placed out of harms reach, away from the rows.

I flew to Canada in December 1994. The GM at the hotel was a delightful guy, but I could imagine the mental turmoil he was going through, having this Englishman sent by the Forte management to his hotel for no obvious reason. Was I to replace him? Was I spying on his efficiency? None of the above, I reckon I was being sent on a jolly 3,560 miles away, seven-and-a-half hours flying time, to keep me out of the way until the designated job became vacant.

I thought the best I could do was enjoy myself and take it all in. The hotel couldn't have done more to make me comfortable. I was treated like a celebrity guest and ate so much good food that for the first time in my life I began to put on weight. I was certainly in the right place as the King Eddie, as it was popularly known, had played host to plenty of top stars in its long history. I went jogging with the GM to try and keep some of the pounds off, but the temperatures were sub-zero and the ground slippery and dangerous. He included me in all the staff meetings and politely asked my advice now and again, but he learned about as much as I did, which wasn't a lot.

At least it kept me away from the politicking back home in England

and for the first time I was going to be able to spend Christmas and New Year with my family when I returned from my "holiday" with lots of gifts bought in my spare time in the Toronto shopping malls.

Despite my little sojourn in Canada, I was still none the wiser about my own future as the GM was still in his position in charge of the Berystede and I was still in limbo. Instead of making a decision, they shunted me off again, this time to the White Horse Hotel in Dorking, as an introduction to the Heritage Group of hotels. This was not the size of hotel to which I was accustomed, with only 78 rooms and run very differently to anything I had been used to with no big budget and no great expectations. Profit margins were tight and there were limitations with what could be done. I was there for six weeks, with my own office wondering what I could do and where would I be going next.

Naturally I was still in touch with a great many friends and colleagues at Grosvenor House, hearing disturbing stories about my replacement and his wife living the high life. In my tenure the only time we wined and dined in the hotel restaurants was when we were entertaining for business, but the new man was residing in one of the top apartments and dining in our Michelin star restaurant with family and friends.

As far as I was concerned it was not my style and privately I felt what he was doing was thieving. I didn't realise how close my prognosis was as within a couple of years he was out of the door. He had been ordering champagne for his apartment and he and his wife were eventually caught taking valuable paintings from the hotel by the watchful security people. I worked with him for a few months during the hand over and my opinion of his was formed then. He was an unpleasant person not fit for the job. Was I bitter? Of course I was.

Meanwhile in Dorking I was learning how not to spend money. It was the difference between the Premier League and the fifth tier of football and whereas I could previously order 500 new chairs or the entire refurbishment of a suite, that was Park Lane, and this was the countryside. Every purchase was scrutinised and more often than not turned down by an accountant rather than someone with knowledge of the hotel industry at the guest level. If someone wet the bed in the Grosvenor, the mattress would be thrown out and replaced, but not with a three star hotel. It had to be dried and used again, as did everything. I spent my six long weeks in Dorking and then, at last, took over as the General Manager at the Berystede.

It took me a while to get used to it as there were no VIP's, no royalty, no Prime Ministers, no sports stars and not the excitement and glamour of a five star hotel in the middle of London. The staff were good and the customers a delight, it was just different.

I also quickly discovered what the delay had been in me taking over. The area manager and the GM I replaced were close friends as well as a working partnership. I wasn't wanted because they thought I was Rocco's blue eyed boy. The GM called me one day and put it to me straight. Was I taking his job or not. What could I say? I knew the man because he had worked at the Grosvenor House when he was front office manager and had worked hard for his promotion to the job I was about to take from him.

It was a pleasant hotel with 91 bedrooms and a decent staff. There were naturally a few who I could see didn't fit in and they were quickly gone, including the chef. The food and beverage man for the group was a real pro and when I told him of my problem with the cheffing with Ascot looming we had to sit down and sort it out. We knew we would be swamped with diners and drinkers, mainly Irish and all of them prepared to spend a great deal of money, especially those who had backed winners! The Irish punters were a great lot who had no inhibitions. I told him I needed someone urgently to fill the gap and he said no problem, he would send along one his best men. I asked who and he told me, Marco Pierre White. He was working closely with the directors at Grosvenor House on all things related and he was undoubtedly the up and coming chef of the time. Of course, I had heard of him and knew his reputation, but I had never met the man.

His arrival was something to behold as he rolled up with two mates straight from a night out fishing. I was a little nervous, knowing of the reputations of these chefs and having sacked a few of them in my time, but what a nice guy he turned out to be.

He introduced me to one of his companions, a head chef from one of his restaurants, who he had seconded to us for the week along with a couple of his assistants. Those chefs he brought in were good, but as hard as nails. They weren't rude, just tough and took no nonsense. "The guest complains that the steak is not cooked properly," said a waiter, "Tell the guest to f*** off," said the chef, "That's the way we do steaks." Marco took the trouble to pop back in to make sure all was well, and I was able to thank him personally. He was a top man and a top cook, the first British chef to be awarded three Michelin stars but was better known by the public for his tyrannical reign over his chefs and kitchens, plus his bad language, there for everyone to see and hear on national television. Speak as you find. I really liked him, and he helped me out at a difficult time.

There is no doubt the Berystede was a luxury hotel and had great potential, indeed they found me a chef after Ascot, and we went on to achieve two AA rosettes. But it was hard to concentrate, knowing I had made an enemy in the area director, and I knew that he was waiting for me to slip up and get me out of the Forte Group. I was also aware that he had the backing of at least one of the directors who also felt threatened by my relationship with Rocco.

It came to head one day when I was overseeing the food for Rocco at the Sunningdale Golf Club down the road, where he was involved in a charity tournament sponsored by Forte plc. I virtually stripped the kitchen and re-erected it at the golf club to serve lunch and then, in the evening, put on a cocktail reception and canapes back at the Berystede, which delighted the guests and Sir Rocco, as he now was.

I had been at the Berystede for exactly two years when Sir Rocco succumbed to a hostile takeover bid by Granada and the Forte empire collapsed. I was to be made redundant after thirty years in the business.

Do Not Disturb

It wasn't just me losing my job as Granada cut the costs before breaking up the group and selling it off in chunks. Instead of having a general manager for each of the five hotels in our group they had just the one to look after all of them until the sale went through. For the first time in my life, I was unemployed. But not for long.

Out of nowhere I took a call from Giuseppe Pecorelli, a former director of Trusthouse Forte who asked me if I was still on the market. I was immediately interested as I had brushed shoulders with him when I was at the Grosvenor House and knew he had started the Exclusive Hotel collection group and by this time he owned four hotels. He was a decent, well liked man and offered me the job as consultant for three months and gave me a list of improvements needed at Pennyhill Park Hotel in Bagshot, Surrey, a hotel I knew well and just a couple of miles down the road from Berystede.

He had suggested we had coffee together when I first moved to Berystede and now he wanted me to meet him to discuss my future and that of Pennyhill Park, which was undergoing some serious renovations after a fire. The general manager had already been made redundant, suffering from stress and I soon dispensed with the deputy general manager and, almost inevitably, a few chefs, and set about proving myself yet again. Within ten days Mr Pecorelli was back on the phone, telling me to forget about the trial period and offering me the contract as general manager there and then.

I didn't go in like a bull in a China shop but wasn't shy of telling him what was wrong and what was needed. It didn't take long to discover that he was losing around £6,000 a week from items which were not being charged to guests' bills alone. Not thieving, just carelessness, with things like bottles of whisky and the like not being added to the bill, and items on the night before check out, not included. I had also noticed that VAT had not been charged to the corporate clients, who claimed it back while it was omitted from our bills. This was worth thousands of pounds which could be used before paying the government at the end of the financial year.

I met him some years later and he told me he admired me for my great tenacity, and he added that I had made him a lot of money from my VAT observations. I was also able to warn him about adding service charges to big events like weddings and then paying to the staff without declaring it. I should have learned from my own advice, as I later became embroiled in the same trap when I opened my own hotel.

I spent over three happy but busy years at Pennyhill Park and I was getting itchy feet to get back to the hustle and bustle of London and quietly let it be known on the grapevine that I was on the lookout for a change of location.

I was getting offers as my situation became known and went to the Carlton Club in London for an interview, where I and one other guy were the last two standing for this prestigious job. The person from the headhunting company who had come to me originally, called and put it to me that I didn't really want the job. He wasn't far from the mark, and I admitted to him that I wasn't sure I was best suited to be a club man and that maybe I was much more of a hotel person.

Mr Pecorelli, who also played his part in my development in the latter years, was delighted when I told him I was going to stay at Pennyhill. But the cat had been let out of the bag and offers continued to come in and I was then offered a job at the Royal Horse Guards Hotel in London by Buckingham Palace, which appealed to my ego and I decided to take.

I should have been warned about bad attitudes and wrong directions before I had my interview when they asked me to take an IQ test! Unbelievable. I didn't take it seriously and instead of walking out and telling them what they could do with their job, I read the ten questions.

I didn't take it seriously to the extent that I gave the opposite answer to what I really thought to each of the ten silly questions. Incredibly, I scored nine and was told it was the highest they had ever had. Me, thick as two short planks, was the best…at guessing what answers they wanted!

Mr Pecorelli and his son Danny tried persuading me to stay again, but I restated my desire to return to London and this time stuck to my guns. When went to say goodbye to Mr Pecorelli he said he wouldn't say goodbye because he knew I would be back with him one day, which turned out to be true.

The hotel's position must have been one of the grandest in the world, situated as it was for Trooping the Colour, the state opening of Parliament and the annual Remembrance Day parade.

The hotel was a big attraction, a beautiful building, a great location and with 280 bedrooms. Sadly the area manager was another accountant with no feel for the real hotel business, just his column of figures. There were immediate restrictions on my spending and obstacles were put in front of me that had never been mentioned at the interview. Had I known what was ahead, I would not have taken the job. Sorry to labour the point but accountants do not know how to run hotels. Control on finance is needed, but experienced general managers know what is needed and it hurts when you have to apologise to a customer because something was not right at their daughter's wedding, and you have to knock something off the bill. Is that good accounting? Is that making the figures balance? I desperately needed more staff, especially on reception, and suggested he came to the hotel one Sunday morning when there was the usual mass exodus, with queues of irritated and anxious guests waiting to settle their bills, keen to get off to catch trains or planes, and there I am with one receptionist, often trying to check out over 150 guests. He declined.

I was there for a year and while I enjoyed it, I did not have a working relationship with the men above me.

It was a shame because there was massive scope and potential for improvement which could have seen the hotel match its prime position in London. There were plenty of my VIPs at this hotel, especially being so close to Downing Street and the Houses of Parliament. There were lots of diplomats and dignitaries, eating, drinking and staying. But there was always this burden of cutting corners, keeping down costs and satisfying the accountants. It could never work under those circumstances, and it was a relief when the persistent Mr Pecorelli came back to me again, stayed the night before going to a West End show and told me outright that this hotel wasn't for me.

I couldn't disagree but he was offering me South Lodge Hotel in Lower Beeding, which had only 41 bedrooms. It was a beautiful property in 93 acres. I was convinced I would be bored with not enough to do. In the end he persuaded me to have a chat with his son Danny. I was on a good salary at the Royal Horse Guards but when Danny put the offer on the table it was one in all honesty I could not refuse, well above the money the Royal Horse Guards were paying me.

I was sad to go but only because I knew I could have turned it round with a free hand, made it the hotel the owners wanted and turned them a very healthy profit. On my last day in Whitehall, I went to bid farewell, not a fond one, to the man who had made my life uncomfortable and restricted my creative juices, in truth I felt like punching him on the nose, but I managed to restrict my assault to a verbal one, telling him that this hotel would never be great again until he was gone.

It was very satisfying, and I was glad I had restrained myself and not pushed him over the table in the lobby. He knew as much about hotels as I did about accounting. Unsurprisingly, he did not survive for much longer.

One of the attractions of South Lodge was that Danny and his father wanted me to oversee the building of a new conference centre, costing £6-8 million with twelve meeting rooms. This was a challenge, and I took into it my beliefs of an emphasis on detail and quality with everything at the highest possible standard and Mr Pecorelli backed me.

In March 2009 the centre was used by the G20 Finance Ministers' Summit and the hotel received a personal letter of thanks from the

Chancellor of the Exchequer, Alistair Darling, praising the facilities. I knew South Lodge like the back of my hand from my days at Pennyhill Park. Mr Pecorelli would call monthly meetings there where we would relay our figures to him. Sometimes for a change of scenery, we would go to the Manor at Castle Coombe, indeed, going to each of the hotels for our meetings to explain our profit and loss round the table with all the general managers. When I was helping the rebuild at South Lodge the meetings were every week. He liked to be kept up to speed. Using what I had learned from Olga Polizzi, I refurbished the hotel's bedrooms and saw the ratings on the AA inspection rise from 72 per cent to 86 per cent and eventually the hotel increased the capacity from the original 40 to 89 and the annual turnover went from £2million a year to £5million. I was involved all along the line, with the colour schemes and everything else connected and my opinion was listened to.

The biggest of the rooms could accommodate a healthy 150 and overlooked the perfect countryside through the picture windows. We built the monster, and it was beautifully done. I had to add on more kitchens to cope with the banqueting and, at first, Mr Pecorelli was concerned because the takings took a nosedive. He wanted to bring people in to show them how things were developing but I was able to persuade him that there was nothing to see until it was finished and then he could bring in the guests to look around and rake in the profits.

I started my first Ladies' Lunch Club at South Lodge and 145 ladies turned up every couple of months to hear a guest speaker and enjoy our food. I enjoyed playing host and within a short while we had a waiting list for every speaker. South Lodge was part of a small village but surrounded by big houses and wealthy people who I wanted to attract, first with the lunch clubs and then to pop in for coffee or drinks and then lunch or dinner. I wanted them to tell their family, tell their friends and this was how the trade was built, no longer just for overnight guests but for the local folk as well. I had to change the staff to suit the new concept, but the chef, Lewis Hamblet, was key to the project and stayed on. He is not only still at South Lodge some 25 years later as I write this, with his wife Haley who is also the Pastry

Chef, and his son Tom Hamblet, the Sous Chef. In December of 2023 the 24-year-old flame haired Tom won the MasterChef Professionals title and looks set to emulate his talented father.

This encouraged me to put on other events with garden parties on the lawn, an annual Big Band concert and open air Shakespeare performances which raised the profile of the hotel and further encouraged non-residents to use the facilities we offered. I understand some hotels keeping their facilities strictly for their guests, but I see the hotels outside the cities being much more the hub of the community.

The Mannings Heath Golf Club was a couple of miles away and a separate entity with two 18-hole championship courses. After three years at South Lodge, Mr Pecorelli asked me if I would manage the facilities there as well as the hotel, as it was making a £350,000 loss. Golf is not my sport and I wondered whether I could connect, but I was able to tighten the reins, and although there was no great profit in it, at least we were able to break even which had to be a result. I have to say I enjoyed working for and with the Pecorelli family and I learned a great deal from Giuseppe. In all I spent four-and-a-half years there and loved it with so many projects to keep me busy there was no time for me to be bored, the one fear I had when I signed the dotted line. I was proud of my achievements and remained involved with the Chase Children's Hospice, the hotel's chosen charity, when I departed.

As happy as I was at South Lodge, I became restless again and all the time nagging away at the back of my mind was the thought of owning and running my own hotel, using my vast store of knowledge with no interference.

I was well aware that the costs were bordering on the prohibitive and it was a big leap from general manager to owner. But I had forty years of experience in the bank and the inspiration of Charles Forte's rise from a single milk bar to heading the world's largest hotel chain. And I had Wendy.

CHAPTER NINE

AND ON TO EASTBOURNE

I promised Giuseppe Pecorelli that I would stay at South Lodge until I retired. But was once again I was becoming restless. It didn't add up, as both Wendy and I were settled in our jobs with mine for the rest of my working life and Wendy working happily as a secretary at a school in Croydon.

I was financially secure, the mortgage on our house was paid off and I could work until I felt it time to put my feet up and go on a cruise or two and long holidays. It all sounded good, but it didn't sound like me and gradually the devil on my left shoulder nudged me towards thinking about the dream of a hotel of my own, while the sensible angel on my right shoulder told me it was nothing more than a pipe dream which could end in financial disaster. Wendy, the real life advisor, just shook her head and said no in several languages.

In 2004 we had bought ourselves a bolthole, a flat on the Sussex coast at Eastbourne Marina, somewhere we could relax together when we had the time. But the idea of my own hotel had taken hold, and, despite Wendy's doubts, I put out feelers about borrowing a large chunk of money and began looking at details of hotels on the market.

Life changed once more when one morning I spotted an advert in the Caterer & Hotelkeeper with a photo of the Langham Hotel a mile or so down the road from our little flat in Eastbourne. It was privately owned, had 85 bedrooms and was on the market for just under £2m, but what really caught my eye was the fantastic location right on the seafront with nothing between the hotel and the sea but the road and the beach.

Looking out to the right was the quintessential Eastbourne Pier and across the bay to the left was the ancient town of Hastings. Clearly there was going to be the need for some decoration both outside and in, and the white plastic chairs on the terrace would have to go. My mind was already working on what I could do to improve it. The building, like a great deal of the seaside town, was Victorian, attractive and reminiscent of the Fortes' home in London and some of those elegant houses in Eaton Square.

The excitement had started to build. My next step was to go and sit outside the hotel on Monday, Wednesday and Saturdays, to get an idea of the footfall, how many visitors were passing by at various times of the day. There was a pedestrian crossing from the hotel to the promenade and I observed the many hundreds of people crossing at that point and heading directly towards the Langham Hotel on their way to town, the local shops or the Royal Hippodrome theatre. I was almost sold on the place already.

The house in Sanderstead was paid for after 23 years, and we had the brand new paid for flat in the newly developed Marina on the outskirts of the seaside town of Eastbourne. I eventually broke the news of my interest in the hotel to a sceptical Wendy who reminded me that I had said if we bought a flat in the harbour, I would stop going on about buying an hotel.

Undeterred, I pointed it out as we walked from our new flat to the pier on a morning stroll. I told her about the potential, the 85 bedrooms and snip at under £2m. Wendy just laughed and asked me where I thought I would get that sort of money, and wasn't impressed when I suggested remortgaging the house, mortgaging the new flat and cashing in one of my pensions. She wasn't laughing any more.

I persuaded her to step inside and have a cup of tea but more pertinently to have a look around. Eventually I talked her round, but it was one hell of a thing to do and was far from just the pair of us saying yes, we will buy it.

The bank was key and wanted a five year business plan which I produced and told them that we would have it refurbished in four years, along with the pigs that were flying past the window at the time. Money was no problem whether it was for a house or a hotel in those heady days through the end of 2004 and into 2005. They were there to lend money and I had a good track record with them financially plus my lengthy background as a successful hotelier, with some well-known names on my Curriculum Vitae.

Wendy, despite her doubts, backed me to the hilt and we both went boldly into it, remortgaging the house, selling the flat and borrowing £150,000 from friends Bob Prodger and his wife Rita, which was to be paid back over five years. I met Bob when I was working for Mr Pecorelli, doing jobs at Pennyhill Park and South Lodge, making chairs to our specification and other furniture to our special requirements. He lived in a big house down the road from South Lodge and I met him for the first time when he had been instructed by the boss, Mr Pecorelli, to meet up with me and discuss the new conference centre. We got be good friends over the years. He was a real nice, down to earth chap with both of us working together to satisfy the will of the boss, leather padded chairs with the hotel logo and all that sort of stuff. He always delivered as promised and on time. I was chatting to him about my new venture and mentioned I was short of cash. He promptly and to my great surprise said he would lend it to me at 7 per cent and was as good as his word. I paid him off every month as undertaken, and it was all done in the promised five years.

We made the offer, £100,000 short of the £1.95m asking price and it was accepted. The Martyr family had enjoyed the property for 92 years but had let the hotel fall into some disrepair.

The history of 43-49 Royal Parade, Eastbourne, is turbulent to say the least and far from being an hotel, it was a series of lodging houses in 1885, with number 49 being the odd one out, owned by Fred Popham a "ship and smack owner." By 1899 it had begun to change with 43 now a boarding house, 44 and 45 apartments, 46 and 47 lodging houses, 48 apartments and 49 still gloriously different and now a "Bookseller's Holiday Home" owned by Geoffrey Larner.

The turn of the century saw more change and by 1911 only Mrs Ellen Eaton remained in 45. Captain Fred Yates had bought and turned 43 into a private home, 44, 45 and 46 were all apartments and 47 and 49, finally succumbing, and now another boarding house. Four years later 43 was, once again, an apartment along with 44, 45 and 46 while 47, 48 and 49 were all boarding houses.

The hotel itself was started in 1911 in a small way and gradually grew as the houses alongside were purchased and the hotel extended by the Martyr family who, in 1939, owned 44, 45 and 47 and by the end of the war they had 44-47, while Miss MacKenzie was the proprietress of the St. Cloud Private Hotel (48-49). It was not until 1958 that the Martyr family were growing the company, owning 48 to 49 and beginning to expand in Royal Parade to what is now our own Langham Hotel.

Six years later planning permission was granted for a four storey extension to 49, followed by planning permission to add floors above 43, with further improvements to the exterior, including the ramp at the front of the hotel and the Entrance Canopy.

I dealt with the son Julian, whose father Tony died in 2002 in the flat where we live now. When I bought the hotel, the mother went into care where she passed on. There was a light moment, a funny story during the build up to buying the hotel. I went for a medical connected to the insurance and found myself face to face with Dr Martyr, wife of Julian from whom we were buying the hotel. I apologised, said I thought I recognised her and that's when I discovered who it was. She gave me a thorough going over, including getting me to drop my trousers and cough.

We both looked at each other and laughed at the coincidence and incongruity of the moment, even before I said she would need to use two hands!

I was up to my eyes in debt, but I owned my own hotel, the journey had been made from washer up in the basement to an hotel with one of the best sea views you could ever wish for.

It was a lot of money, however you looked at it, and Wendy was far more daunted than me when she did the maths and saw it well short of the £1,850,000 I eventually paid for the Langham Hotel.

She saw the enormous amount of work that it would need to bring it up to scratch while I saw this busy Victorian architecture, with echoes of the elegant residences in Eaton Square. I believed the potential was enormous. At least to me it was. What also stimulated me was the footfall with thousands of potential customers strolling to and from their hotels; off to the beach; queueing at the ice cream kiosks; heading for the slots on the pier or just ambling into Eastbourne town for some lunch or shopping.

There was a zebra crossing right outside the hotel where, every few minutes a line of cars would come to a halt with the views of the sea on one side and our hotel on the other. Most seemed to look at the hotel as they passed whether in car or on foot, viewing the people sitting enjoying a cocktail or a coffee or to check the time on the big hotel clock.

I also fell into conversation with a few of the passers-by and those on the terrace and most had good words to say about the hotel, but all agreed it had slipped a lot in recent times, that the enthusiasm there previously had dissipated when it was learned the premises were up for sale.

Wendy and I also checked inside and found the barman sitting reading a novel and when we asked him if we could order sandwiches and a drink, we were told the chef was off duty and there was nobody in the kitchen. That was a few more pounds lost, and no one seemed bothered.

It didn't put me off, only encouraged me to think how much better I could do it. I had looked at what else was available and the position and the view were enough to convince me, especially the view. But I needed to know a lot more and, adopting my best Inspector Clouseau guise, I persuaded a few of my friends to check the hotel out, have a drink, dinner, stay the night, try the breakfast and all the other things a weekend visitor might do. I didn't want to know about holes in the carpet, spiderwebs on the cornices or even if the food was rubbish. I was more interested in the service because that is what a hotel lives or dies on. There was a sign outside advertising weddings but when one of my accomplices asked, the Duty Manager responded that they no longer did weddings and when my secret agent pressed, he was asked when they planned the nuptials, he replied July, to which the Duty Manager said smugly that they were full in July.

Another Mystery Guest stayed late at the bar where there were more staff than customers and not only were they all drinking, but there was also no money going into the till. I knew I could turn that and the other problems around with an upgrade of staff and decided to make my offer.

It was accepted at the second attempt, and I was now the owner of the Langham Hotel, Royal Parade on the Eastbourne seafront. One of the first I told was Sir Rocco Forte. "Welcome to the club," he said with some scepticism.

Wendy had swallowed her doubts as was four-square behind me and that was all I needed.

The contracts were signed on Friday 1st July 2005. It was the Chinese Year of the Rooster and I was crowing. The former washer-upper now owned his own hotel, the AA three-star Langham Hotel and I popped the champagne corks in celebration while Wendy counted up the debts.

We had remortgaged the family home in Sanderstead to the tune of £400,000, well below the market value, remortgaged our flat in Eastbourne Marina; cashed in a pension; withdrew all my savings; and borrowed £150,000 from Bob the furniture man; plus a £1.3 million loan from a smiling bank manager.

It was a heavy debt burden, but everyone had bought into our feasibility plans, and it was now sink or swim. I told Danny Pecorelli at South Lodge the next day and he gave me no grief at all other than ensuring I was going to work my three months notice while they found a replacement. It would have been unfair to leave him in the lurch but it meant that Wendy, who quit her job with Croydon Council on 30th June, would have to run the business on her own while I was away, making her debut as general manager.

I worked five days a week until my notice ran out in October but was back often enough to start sacking the people who were dragging the business down and looking out for my sort of people to replace them. It was a terrible burden to place on Wendy who worked from 7am until we sat down to dinner, or should that be supper, at 11pm.

While I was swanning around at South Lodge, she not only had to oversee the housekeeping, handle the guests needs, manage the staff and bank the cheques, but also had to suffer the slings and arrows from those who knew they were on their way out, regularly leaving her in tears.

To add to her woes, the lift broke down, the ovens malfunctioned, and we both lost weight with neither of us carrying any excess to start with. There was no computerisation in the hotel and there was a lack of communication between departments, with guests arriving with bookings made six months earlier but no record of them anywhere.

But who do you blame? We were the owners, so it had to be us. Our hours were so long, Wendy in the hotel and me on the road to and from South Lodge, we decided it would save time if we moved lock, stock and barrel into the hotel, even though it meant Wendy was chained to it 24 hours a day and on her own for much of that time. It did not help her that when I was back, I was firing incompetents and troublemakers, who often ganged up against my wife in my absence. They were the first in my sights and most of them quickly realised it was a fight they were not going to win and resigned before I could sack them.

Gradually it came together as I finally left South Lodge on excellent terms and began to put together the team I wanted. The first job was to appoint a new general manager. No choice. It was me. The next task was to relieve Wendy of some of the burden I had left her with as I worked my notice. My daughter Nicola took over the accountancy; son David became a chef and Wendy got the housekeeping shipshape before moving on to her area of expertise, the administrative side.

I knew in my mind's eye exactly how I wanted the Langham Hotel to be, using my store of experience from the other hotels where I worked to mould it the way I wanted. It meant Wendy and I working all hours God sent but it was worth it then and now.

First task to be tackled was the lobby area, after all this is the first place every guest saw when they walked in through the front door, and they would carry that influence with them throughout their stay and when they left. It needed to look as professional as the staff sat behind it. As it was the carpet was badly frayed and the desk was outdated. We gutted it totally and raised the ceiling by two feet to stop it feeling so claustrophobic after coming in off the sea front.

The first phase went as I hoped except for one slight glitch. My son-in-law James helped me with the demolition of the old desk, which was made up of breeze blocks and chicken wire. His enthusiasm and strength were commendable, until he got carried away and chipped a large piece of concrete off the block. It whistled past my head and sliced into my arm, leaving a large gash and lots of blood. It required hospital and eight stitches. The scar remains as a reminder of those hairy first days.

But the transformation was truly remarkable. Remembering Olga Polizzi's insistence on only the best, I had a solid oak reception desk hand made, installed crystal chandeliers, wood panelling to dado height, new carpeting, custom made chairs and sofa, with much of it done by master craftsman Bob Prodger, with his wife Rita selecting suitable art work to go with his craftsmanship. Careful selection of table lamps, shades and wallpaper made sure the rich colours blended together with another of Olga Polizzi's doctrines of matching dark wood with deep red bringing it all together.

The final touch was a magnificent wooden key rack for reception with pigeon holes for each room number, all designed and carved by Bob. My final touch was to order a bust of my hero Sir Winston Churchill from the Imperial War Museum to overlook all who came and left my hotel. I kept all of our clients updated with a scheme board and photographs of how it would look when finished and they all seemed to buy into the project and looked forward to returning to witness the progress.

Next in line was the main restaurant and that too was redecorated and re carpeted over a five day period while Wendy and I designed some stained glass window panels, made locally depicting local scenes and chairs made for height and comfort while new china, glasses, cutlery and table linen were purchased. We followed with the total restoration of the adjoining Portico Restaurant where we laid a new oak floor, elegant lighting and smart black blinds. With its magnificent vistas of the sea viewed through the large windows, we renamed it The Conservatory and turned it into an a la carte restaurant which quickly became established when we appointed Michael Titherington as Head Chef.

By 2009, we became the only hotel in Eastbourne to boast an AA rosette for our food. Michael was more than just the head chef as he was married to Claire, the head receptionist, in the hotel! He is now the deputy general manager behind the GM Simon Brown.

For many years the AA and RAC were accepted arbiters of the quality of hotels and the food they served. Times change and customers will now take their recommendations from the internet from sites like Trip Advisor.

I eventually abandoned the AA as the costs no longer justified the end product while the once eagle-eyed inspectors seemed to me to lack the knowledge and the experience to make what could be crucial judgements. Having raised our standards to earn an AA rosettes for our food and four stars for the hotel, I made the decision to quit the relationship with the AA.

The sign came down and not a single person, customer or otherwise, ever commented. It was costing me around £3,000 a year for something which had become stale. I have nothing against the inspectors, they were generally pleasant people but there was little or no return for my investment. I finally decided enough was enough when I engaged one of their operatives in conversation asking her what her background was in the hotel trade. She had been involved in housekeeping, nothing wrong with that coming from an ex-dishwasher, and she had used her expertise to point out some hair under a plug in a shower in one of the rooms, and a dusty corner in another room.

On this basis she told me she was not going to give me any more points. I didn't lose my temper but quietly explained that since the last examination I had spent £650,000 improving all the bedrooms and she was going to leave me on the same points. I suggested she look at our clients' reviews and then explain to her bosses why I pulled out after her inspection.

Frankly I didn't need their reviews anymore, they were wasting my time and were of no further use in the face of competition like TripAdvisor. When I first arrived at the Langham there were the two signs hanging outside, the AA and the RAC, with the latter stopping their inspections, leaving the AA a clear run. We were delighted when we attained our fourth star but there seemed to be nowhere to go from there.

We were awarded a Blue Ribbon Award for food voted for by our customers and although we offered to stay with the AA for the food rosettes, they said we had to be a member of the entire thing and couldn't have one without the other. No thanks. Move on.

We also climbed back on the wedding bandwagon and prospective clients were awestruck by the honeymoon suite which we created by knocking a single room and a twin into one on the first floor. It gave a large, elegant space with magnificent views across the bay. I wanted this to be the best, most luxurious hotel suite in town. We had a four poster bed made specially, red carpets, a chandelier and sophisticated Zoffany wallpaper to give the room exactly the ambience I wanted. It was reflected in the speed the wedding diary filled up.

The kitchens followed with the latest ovens and equipment, walk-in freezers, the lot. The bar underwent a complete makeover. The ceiling was raised, and walls knocked down and specially designed cornices and solid wood panelling replaced the dowdy old fittings and new furniture graced the luxurious red carpet. The bar counter, made of black granite, complimented the array of black and white photographs.

I also got rid of the awful white plastic chairs on the terrace, replacing them with silver and black chairs with proper tables and black umbrellas, complete with a canopy declaring it was "Langhams Bar" to attract the interest of all those passing by on their promenade along the prom.

The changes were astonishing and created exactly the atmosphere I had dreamed of in those early days. Not only the hotel changed but so did the patrons. When I took it over 98 per cent of the business was coach parties and as the private guests grew in numbers, I was able to plough the income back into the business to improve it even further. Not all of it was visible, with important features like a new fire alarm system and washing machines and tumble dryers installed, but they could see and enjoy the recarpeting of the corridors, the new lighting and, in the basement area the embarrassing staff bedrooms were converted into three conference rooms with an additional bar.

It is all a bit like painting the Forth Bridge because no sooner is one task complete than another comes into view. The sea air is invigorating and healthy but is also extremely corrosive with the salt eating away at the outside façade. That is all part of running a resort hotel, so different to an establishment in the middle of the posh part of

London. But, in the end, it is the people inside that make it a good or a poor hotel, the owners, the staff and, naturally, the customers because without them we have nothing at all. They pay our wages, as I keep telling my team.

Staffing the hotel from the highest position to the lowest, all of which I have savoured, remained a priority and I was especially pleased when I asked my old friend Andrew Coy to join me and he accepted, taking over my role as General Manager to free me for my duties as an owner. He made the giant leap from London's finest to the Langham in 2012 and spent just over three years with me.

Our relationship went back a long way as I first met him as banqueting director at Grosvenor House. Here was a man with a fabulous CV and undoubtedly the best banqueting manager I have ever met or worked with, handling 2000 covers in one sitting at Grosvenor House. He is probably the best in Europe, certainly in the UK, having worked at the Ritz, Savoy, Grosvenor House, Royal Horseguards, Café Royal and the Langham Hotel Eastbourne.

I first came across him when Forte brought him to the hotel when I was apartments manager. It was a massive job, handling up to 2,000 covers in the Great Room plus another 500 in the Ballroom, an absolute money spinner providing it was handled properly, a very important job within the entire group, hence why Sir Rocco Forte brought him in from the Cafe Royal at the time. It was a big job and the general manager Matt Buccianti wasn't keen on the appointment only to be overruled by Rocco himself. GM's as a general rule don't like being told who they should appoint by the board of directors but that's life, shut your mouth and get on with it. Andrew was not a rebel by any stretch of the imagination, but he insisted on doing a lot of things his own way, that's why he was so good. It was alright for his General Manager going home to the wife and dinner at 6.45pm while Andrew rarely left for home before 2am when all was done and cleared up after another major, money-spinning event. He stayed six nights a week, not going home until the seventh day.

Do Not Disturb

When I bought the Langham Hotel, I contacted him and asked if he would come in as general manager. I was exhausted and needed some help and it allowed me to assume my proper role as proprietor. I was delighted when he said yes and couldn't wait to give it a shot. We were good friends and knew how each other worked and he relished the challenge. He did a great job in the three years he worked with me and, amazingly, we didn't fall out or anything like that.

But he is a restless soul, always up for fresh challenges and when he was offered a new job, he was ready to go, parting with a firm handshake. He was always of the opinion that three or four years was a good spell in a job, whether as banqueting manager or general manager. Eventually he left to run his own business, Simply Banqueting, doing lots of work for a variety of top customers, including the Rugby Football Union. He also trains butlers around the world, even being featured on television showing how he trained these people for America, Russia and, of course, the Arab billionaires. He would train them up to a high standard and then send them off for their new appointments.

We are both busy by nature and choice and while the friendship remains, there is not a lot of time to socialise, although I did invite him down to Eastbourne to run a spot check over the hotel for me. He is a great food and beverage man and while we had moved it forward, I wanted him to run the rule over the operation, the food, the service and standards. We all get stale, and I wanted him to come up with some new ideas to help me maintain the progress. I have always respected him and do so to this day.

More recently I asked him to come over and stay at the hotel while my restaurant manager was on maternity leave, but home commitments precluded another get together, which would have been to my benefit. He also had a new hip like me, but not through running the roads, more like rushing around restaurants and banqueting rooms. An honest, hardworking, loyal man who could handle a million pound Saudi wedding or a celebrity dinner with the same degree of skill and professionalism.

He had to be on the ball all the time, doing something the GM couldn't always do, able to synchronise over a hundred waiters to move as one to serve between 1,500 and 2,000 diners.

It was big, big money for Fortes because apart from the hire of the room, the dinner, the wine and all that went with it, the hosts would frequently take up to a hundred rooms as well. It was a money tree.

My love/hate relationship with weddings switched yet again while Andrew was with me and we stopped doing weddings in 2017 completely because they were becoming too gross. Too many of the guest went silly on the free drinks they were served: misbehaving, throwing up everywhere and becoming boisterous. The class of the clientele was not always what we had hoped for, many of the weddings were done as cheaply as possible and this was reflected in the bride and groom and their guests, who arrived suited and booted and behaving well, only to decline into something else altogether, real Jekyll and Hyde. The tie is pulled down, the jacket comes off and there is white powder on the sinks in the toilets.

They were vastly different from the elegant, sophisticated weddings we arranged at Pennyhill and the other venues. Not all were like that, but enough to spoil it for others, taking up the restaurant which was another constant source of income. Our downstairs room is small by comparison with a maximum of 38 guests for the wedding breakfast and no room for dancing until we cleared out all of the chairs.

The two groups did not mix well in the evening, either with one group quietly settling down for dinner while the other group, more often than not, let us all know they were still there and up for more.

In the end and after a discussion with Andrew Coy, we decided to switch from weddings to Masonic ladies' festival weekends. It was a great decision at the time with guests often staying for two nights and up to 90 attending, this against a couple of rooms for the wedding including the Bridal Suite and rooms for mum and dad.

Do Not Disturb

If there was a separate function room and lawns for the kids to run around it would have been different, but we were restricted, and the weddings had to go. Financially it was a good decision as we made a great deal of money with the Lodges.

They ran for nine or ten years before Covid came along and killed the business. After the pandemic they contacted me but were talking about half the numbers which tilted the balance the other way, from healthy profit to break even. Now we do neither weddings nor ladies festivals, and I don't regret either as we are increasing our private clientele all of the time. We are close to full at weekends even in the winter months, with around 85 eating in the restaurant, both residents and non-residents. The honeymoon suite is now a luxury suite and the four poster beds have been removed. They were in fact too successful in the aims and ambitions, encouraging couples to make full use of the facilities. In consequence anyone unfortunate enough to be in the room below, particularly the honeymoon suite, which was over reception, could tell exactly when the horizontal games were taking place as the ceilings shook and the chandeliers jangled. The one above reception would go into a Highland Fling with the girls looking up and commenting that they were at it in room 112.

We refurbished the suites to make them even better, spending £15,000 per room, with new carpets and curtains and a kingsize bed on which they could frolic all they liked without disturbing the peace.

We have invested a further £2 million over past decade in refurbishments, building an even stronger team, adding another dozen employees to the roster, taking the total to almost 60 as against the 27 when I first moved in. We have upgraded the menu in content and style, going from two star to four AA star and continued to improve our market. We started with 98 per cent coach trade and have reduced that to 24 per cent, with the rest private bookings.

That can only be done with refurbishment, higher standards, attention to detail, customers remaining king – but on an equal share with my staff.

We have rewired the place with an expenditure of £300,000 on new fire alarms, electrics, replumbing. We have gone back and refurbished the rooms for a second time, spending another £350,000 in January 2023, upgrading the seaview suites to an even higher standard along with the cutlery, china and uniforms, all raised to a new level.

What is important is that I have the entire team thinking like a five star London hotel. We train them and they work hard as a team. It is not easy to pull so many individuals together, but I believe we have managed it.

The final requirement is for the customer to say how much they loved staying with us when they leave and subsequently returning to stay with us again because they enjoyed it so much.

I hear all the time that we are by far and away the best hotel in Eastbourne. I would say that, wouldn't I? However, I don't need to make it up and that is very satisfying. To maintain this level, it needs to constantly change, never being satisfied and to do this, I listen to the staff and the clients and when they make suggestions for improvements, I try them out. An example is breakfast in the restaurant, although I do not get in the chef's way to try to assist in the cooking, I do serve the tables and listen to what is being said. If they work, then fine, if not thank you and goodnight.

Nothing leaves the kitchen for the table unless it is hot when it should be hot. I introduced smoked salmon and scrambled eggs, omelettes and muffins without adding to the charge. I don't charge separately for the breakfasts, whatever is ordered off the menu carries no extra charges, it is all included in the overnight stay. This, I am aware, is not common practice but it is something I believe in, along with not adding on arbitrary service charges.

The restaurant is such an essential part of our business, and I was quite happy to splash out on a stylish carving trolley, a cheese board and the spectacular fire display of a crepe suzette trolley. Bit much for a restaurant of our size? Not at all. When I worked as a part-time

Do Not Disturb

waiter, I used to don my white gloves and push the trolley out to the table where the waiter would take over the theatrical service. I loved it and wanted to introduce a similar service to our patrons. They love it at our jazz lunches and the cheese board always comes out on a Saturday night.

The sea air is beautiful and bracing but it is also extremely corrosive, and we have already painted the outside for second time, installed a new state of the art wi-fi system for £25,000. As a result of all of this extra effort our occupancy has increased along with our room rates. Moreover, the demand been maintained despite the outside problems thrown at us.

The lunch clubs have never stopped growing, with a waiting list for every experience – whether it is an ABBA Tribute, a Murder Mystery Lunch or Gourmet Lunch. All 100 covers are sold every time and there is a waiting list of over 50 for every event. We have had some great speakers at our lunch clubs over the years, Anita Harris is a great favourite, as well as David (Diddy) Hamilton, Graham Cole and Richard Griffin who was Personal Protection Officer to Her Majesty the Queen and Prince Philip.

We also do a tongue-in-cheek pantomime every festive season all put on by the staff and with the staff, including the most senior staff (i.e. Wendy and me making fools of ourselves), and these are enormously popular. No sooner had we finished the 2023 season than we sold out all of the eight shows for the 2024, with only a handful of seats remaining for the other one as we moved into January. These sorts of occasions bring in not only regular residents but also local people. We try to give them great service, great food and they also get to know the staff and build a rapport with them as well. They know who the vegetarian is, who likes what for dessert and they remember, to the customer's delight and surprise, their birthdays and anniversaries, because we spy on them, making relevant notes for future visits so there is a card or something waiting for them. That is the attention to detail that makes a difference and keeps the customer happy and coming back.

Neil Kirby

Lunch Club guests watching as the Olympic Torch passes Langham Hotel before the London Games July 2012.

Do Not Disturb

The ever popular Langham Staff Pantomime in 2023. From left to right: Kevin Sturt – AV technician, Simon Brown – Genie, Sue Sweeney – Sue Chef, Neil - Chop Suey, Paula Pout – Jasmine, Wendy – Aladdin, Barney Pout – Widow Twankey.

How long will I keep coming back is a different matter, still to be discussed, still to be decided.

Guiseppe Pecorelli advised me to pack in at 72 years of age. He did and passed on his business to his son Danny, who has carried on the good work. Unfortunately, I have no one in the family amongst my three children who is interested in taking on this immense job.

It would be nice if one of my three children fancied carrying on the Kirby name in the industry, but I would be the last person to try to force them. As it is I am proud of them all and we are still friends. My dad always warned me that when they left the nest things could change. A few wrinkles, of course, but nothing to rock the boat.

Nicola was the first born, planned and delivered in October 1978 as hoped for. How lucky was that! I was bemused at how we had to go to bed when the time was right when I just thought then that you had your fun, and the baby came nine months later. We were blessed with a lovely little girl now a lovely lady.

Neil Jnr followed a couple of years later. He was one year old when we moved to Sanderstead. I was delighted when he proved to be a nice little footballer and a runner, like me. I didn't force him to play football or to run but it must have been in the genes. He looked after his sporting career without too much help from me. He went to Miami University on a soccer scholarship, became a personal trainer, worked at LA Fitness in Purley and then at Selsdon Park Hotel and has since done well for himself, forming his own running company, UK Ultra.

We always said we would be happy with a girl and a boy, but we were further blessed when David came along six years after Neil and he is now the only member of the family working at the hotel. They are all very different and we wouldn't have it any other way. At the last count we were up to seven grandchildren.

The mortgage will be paid off in full soon and that will be the time to start making decisions or at least thinking about retirement. It will coincide with my 75th year in November 2027. We will reflect on whether Wendy and I want to get out, where we are with the business and whether we can continue to develop ideas. To carry on a successful business you cannot stand still, you have to make improvements with things like another kitchen building for the bar, continuing to upgrade the bedrooms.

The only alternative would be if someone came along and offered silly money. That would be a tempter but not yet awhile.

Neil Kirby

Family picture celebrating Dad's 99th birthday.

CHAPTER TEN

I DO LIKE TO BE BESIDE THE SEASIDE

All things being equal, Eastbourne was a very good choice not only for the hotel but for our lifestyle. There are no regrets. They reckon it is the sunniest place in England and it's hard to disagree when I sit in my lounge and see the sunshine sparkling off the sea.

I have always told people that I bought the Langham Hotel for the view and certainly it remains one of the features with an unspoiled panorama stretching from Hastings to my left and the magnificent South Downs to the right, sandwiched in between is a resort which plays hosts not only to holiday makers but an entire new community from around the world, all living in peace and harmony apart from a few scallywags, the sort of low life you will sadly always find in seaside resorts.

Is there anywhere more beautiful than the South Downs where, long before we moved, Wendy and I would enjoy the wind blowing in our faces off the sea as we walked or enjoyed the Downs and Beachy Head? I have completed the Eastbourne marathon and the half marathon a few times and never tire of the air and the sights.

Perhaps the best time in Eastbourne is at sunrise and whether I am running, walking or simply gazing out of my flat windows in the Langham, there is no finer sight than looking to the left and watching the sun rise, seemingly out of the sea itself.

We have no neighbours, only the sea, its fishes and the raucous sea gulls, occasionally people bathing and children on holiday playing in perfect, safe surrounds with two lane Royal Parade safely separated from the sunbathers and their families by a stout wall. The promenade is the ideal, old-fashioned stroll, turn left out of the hotel and it is a mile and a half to the Marina, with its boats, restaurants and bars and where we originally bought a flat to enjoy our retirement before I went into debt to become the hotel owner. Turn right past the pier and then the busiest bandstand in Europe, so they claim, and on to Beachy Head which is two and a half miles as the herring gull flies.

There is so much beach that you can join in the buzz from the pier to the bandstand or walk in either directions to find your own spot and bathe or soak up the sun with an ice cream or a bar always within easy reach.

Eastbourne is big enough to swallow the thousands who travel from all over the country and, indeed, the continent these days, without ever feeling crowded. The only time you are shoulder to shoulder is when they put on the four day airshow, surely one of the greatest free shows of the summer, as all eyes turn upwards to watch history in the shape of the Lancaster bomber, the Spitfire and the Hurricane as well as the more modern flying machines from all over and acrobatic teams that will make your skin tingle.

The showpiece remains the spectacular Red Arrows formation team who are the centrepiece of this display which brings folk back year after year. The town is geared up to them, with a vast selection of restaurants and bars offering every type of food, drink and every flavour you can imagine of ice cream and, if you are my age, a few you couldn't imagine.

Of course, I want us to be the best, but it has saddened me to see how many of my competitors have downgraded since Covid. It means customers have a much narrower choice and while that obviously helps me to increase my bookings, competition with better hotels, restaurants and amenities improves Eastbourne generally and attracts more holidaymakers and tourists to what is a beautiful seaside resort which could be so much better. But that requires the sort of investment I have made in making the Langham Hotel much more than just that beautiful view which attracted me initially.

It hurts to walk towards the town towards the Pier and see how much needs to be done. It is the council as well as the private landlords who need to up their game, repair the potholes making the pavements safer, police the town to keep it safe and bring buildings, both public and private, up to date. I even saw a tree growing out of one hotel's roof and then I read the council had stopped the payments to the local Punch and Judy man who gave traditional pleasure on the sea front to children.

It is a shame because Eastbourne is a lovely place and with the potential to be a lot better but it has got worse and worse over the years. Look at the South Downs, Beachy Head, the miles of beach, there is so much to appreciate and enjoy. A little investment can go a long way and make it better and a help to all of us.

What I have found living here is nice friendly people, supportive of the local businesses and when I opened my doors to the locals they embraced the hotel, its amenities and sometimes me as well! With such natural views from our terrace, there is no place better to sit, whether it is to watch the Air Show, the fleet of little yachts, the marathon runners, the long-distance swimmers, the little Dotto train which chugs past during the summer months or our fireworks on the beach on New Year's Eve, we have rowing clubs, swimming clubs who swim to the pier and back and in winter they pop in to warm themselves up with a hot coffee and homemade flapjack.

Eastbourne people are generous folks which is important to me as I like to use my running to help raise money for charity. My latest venture is to run 50k on a treadmill at the hotel, bidding to become the first over-70 to do so. This is a follow up to my first World record in 2022 when I ran a treadmill marathon in four hours 26 minutes. The latest effort is for Sir Jackie Stewart's Running for Dementia, set up when his wife was afflicted with the disease.

A triple hernia operation did not help with my preparations but my background of 51 marathons, including 19 London, and 218 half marathons. During that time I have raised £385,000 and hope to soar beyond £400k after the 50k.

Running my own hotel, raising money for a friend's charity, backed by the generous people of Eastbourne. It doesn't get much better than that.

My running career also brought unexpected privileges. I believe I am officially allowed to herd my sheep over Southwark Bridge as a Freeman of the City of London. Well, at least I would if I had any sheep, plus the inclination to disrupt the London traffic even more than mayor Sadiq Khan!

Although I no longer work or live in London, my association goes back to my childhood and the large part of my working life, but the honour bestowed on me by the Lord Mayor of the City of London on 21st April in the 53rd year of Queen Elizabeth II, was all to do with my charitable work. This includes my continued attempt to raise £400,000, running for charity in London and other marathons and long distance races and, these days, mainly by running many miles overlooking the glorious beaches of my home in Eastbourne

I am still not sure of exactly what the honour permits me to do, but I am well aware of the history and tradition of being awarded the Freedom of the City of London, something which began way back in 1237 and has continued through the ages.

I attended Guildhall with my dad George, then 98, and his lady Doreen and, of course, my lady Wendy. We were given a glass of sparkling wine in the ornate Guildhall where we had lunch and the Mayor, Sir Robert Gerard Finch, and the Chamberlain, Peter Derrick, who presented me with my scroll which proclaimed me as someone who held the Freedom of the City of London.

In old fashioned terms, it means that I am a free man and not under the jurisdiction of a feudal lord. Thank goodness for that, but it is hugely symbolic, which has a long association with privileges in the governance of the City of London going back centuries.

Do Not Disturb

George and Doreen join Neil and Wendy to celebrate Neil receiving the Freedom of London from the Lord Mayor.

There is also an Honorary Freedom of the City of London, given to those with a somewhat higher international profile than I, such as William Pitt the Elder, several members of our royal family, including the late Queen Elizabeth and Prince Philip, as well as our current Monarch, Charles III, the late Diana, Princess of Wales, Sir Winston Churchill and several Prime Ministers, as well as foreign royalty, five presidents of the United States, international leaders, and other such notables as Lord Robert Baden-Powell, Lord Kitchener, Florence Nightingale, Luciano Pavarotti, Morgan Freeman, Sir Michael Caine, Dame Judi Dench and Tommy Steele.

All very grand and it was a lovely day for the four of us, with George bursting with pride. I admit that the notation until recently was in a carrier bag upstairs in the hotel. I am not into showing off. I am sure there are a great many people who have been given the honour for their charity work and it is nice to be one of them without shouting it from the rooftops. But now I know a little more about it I will cherish it.

I was every bit as delighted in February 2024 with the chance to meet one of my boyhood heroes, Sir Geoff Hurst, the last surviving member of the victorious 1966 England World Cup winning team, the main man who scored a memorable hat trick. I attended a talk given by him at the Devonshire Park Theatre in Eastbourne and he kindly signed a copy of his England shirt for me and that will hang in the Langham in a very prominent place.

A charming man who had time for everyone including my two guests, my friend Carl and the executive chef's daughter, Maisee, who both had shirts signed. It was his final tour, and I couldn't miss the opportunity. His story telling was excellent, as were the Q&A session afterwards.

As Alf Garnett was often heard to say: "It was West Ham what won the World Cup, with Geoff, Bobby Moore and Martin Peters." He wasn't wrong, was he?

Sir Geoff Hurst signed my 1966 World Cup Winners shirt in February 2024.

I love Eastbourne. Granted, it is England and it rains. No surprise there, and even though we have more sunshine hours than other resorts on the English coast, we still have to cater for people when it rains. As well as the multiplex cinema and a fabulous indoor shopping centre, we are fortunate to have five theatres to entertain with shows, some on their way to or from London's West End, tribute bands and original drama presented by touring companies and our own thespians.

Another free show which has folk staring open mouthed into the sky above the pier is the murmuration of starlings, one of nature's most beautiful moving tapestries. For those of you unaware of this mesmerising vision, it consists of thousands upon thousands of starlings, similar to the common blackbird, together in flight as a flock, sweeping across the sky in their numbers, swooping, ducking and diving like one single harmonized whole. Murmuration is what the behaviour is called, and it is replicated all over Europe as well as in America where there are reckoned to be over 200 million of these sweetly singing birds. They sleep on the pier at night before resuming their never-ending hunt for food.

There are several parks to cater for all from the kids, to an open-air theatre in the summer, one with a lake where they can safely sail their model boats and within reach of the rides, putting greens and two bowls clubs.

I would also describe it as a "fit" town, I have never seen so many runners and walkers in one area going past my hotel, morning, afternoon and into the night. There are definitely more women than men, probably a ratio of around three to one. They feel safe running along the prom, especially now the fad for the dangerous e-scooter enhanced with a powerful engine, has been and gone, peaking during the pandemic where they were a danger to life and limb. You are more likely to be knocked over by a motorised wheelchair which can be as easily hired as a deckchair.

The schools in the town are excellent both private and state run, with three of my grandchildren going to the state-run schools in Eastbourne with excellent teachers and facilities.

It has been sad to see a reduction in the number of hotel rooms for holidaymakers, with too many closing down after the Covid pandemic, but there are two four star hotels, the Langham and the Hydro, plus the Grand Hotel, which is a Five Black Star.

For those not aware of the finer points of hotel stars, the highest you can get is the Five Red Star, the highest accolade you can get from the AA, hotels in London like the Savoy, Claridge's, Connaught, Dorchester, Grosvenor House and many country house hotels, like

Do Not Disturb

my former employers at Pennyhill Park and South Lodge. These are top of the league, then you have the Five Black Star hotels, like the Grand in Eastbourne. Most people don't realise that there is a big difference between the Red and the Black rated hotels. It's all about service, quality and food and the standard, imagine the Savoy or the Dorchester, beautiful hotels with near perfect service. You can't compare the Grand hotels in Eastbourne and Brighton, for example, with the best London hotels, the difference between having your shoes blacked and cleaned by a valet to using a greased paper glove provided to clean your own. The other difference is, of course, what you pay. The cost of the top room in the top Five Red Star hotels is hugely different to the Black Star.

The most expensive room in London, indeed the entire UK, as I write this chapter, is the £62,000 a night suite at Claridge's. It has four bedrooms plus a swimming pool spreading over the entire roof above the bedrooms, plus a dance floor with a pianist's pavilion, its own wine cellar, dining space for ten and its own lake with a 360 degree panoramic view over London, not to mention original artwork. There is a bonus, stay four nights and get the fifth free! Perhaps free is the wrong word in this instance.

Before that the Lanesborough boasted the most expensive room at a give-away £32,000 a night! Twenty-four-hour butler and maid service plus chauffeur driven Rolls Royce and Bentley's for the shops, restaurants and airports.

I was happy to reach four stars before I pulled out of the dated AA scheme, happy to save the fees and put the cash back into the hotel.

Although the number of quality hotel rooms have diminished in Eastbourne, there has been an increase in flats and apartments to be rented, some of them at a high standard. The Marina has good flats in a pleasant setting.

It seems Eastbourne's unspoilt promenade and Victorian pier make it an ideal site for period locations. Made in Dagenham was a feel-good film about the female equal pay activists at the Essex Ford factory in 1968 and featured scenes shot on Eastbourne seafront and the Langham Hotel. It was originally going to be called 'The Dagenham Girls' but was changed to 'Made in Dagenham' before it went on public release.

The film makers came to the town in August 2010 and set up camp at the Langham and also closed off a section of seafront during filming. They filmed scenes inside and outside the hotel and an 80-strong crew stayed with us. I think they chose the hotel because they liked the 60s style of the building and the original street lights and zebra crossing outside. They changed the name of the hotel, cleared away all our plants and parked their own 1960s cars along the street. It was nice to be part of it.

Do Not Disturb

Made in Dagenham being filmed outside the Langham Hotel in August 2010.

Neil Kirby

Film production of the movie Made in Dagenham outside Langham.

CHAPTER ELEVEN

WE BOUGHT IT FOR THE VIEW

My initial target when I bought the Langham Hotel in 2005 was to raise its profile by taking it from a two star establishment to four stars. This was down to yours truly. It was me and not Wendy who had all of those years in the hotel business in London and I had to translate that experience into the practical running of the hotel. There were lots of tears, lots of hard work and many changes in the staff. If we were going to succeed, I had to be ruthless. I also couldn't do it without a strong team behind me, going from the 27 when I first arrived, to 60 at our peak, before external troubles, such as Covid, intervened and forced us to drop our numbers to 54.

From the outset, the staff had to understand about the service and the quality of a five star hotel. They had no idea of what that was because they had not worked in that end of the industry. I had and knew exactly what I wanted. I had to train them myself on how to speak to customers and how they reacted to any given situation. We all have a duty, including me, to be polite and courteous whenever we are in the public areas. Away from that they could do what they liked as far as I was concerned, providing it was never to the detriment of the hotel.

We had to make sure we had that spot on to encourage customers to come back after the reduction of the coach business. Growing the business to cater for private guests is important because there is more money there. To encourage this, I had to keep upgrading the hotel with a spend of almost £3 million over the course of nearly twenty years and while you could have beautiful room with gold taps, it was wasted if you didn't have the staff to look after you and serve you in the proper manner.

It is not all stiff collar, far from it. The guests love a bit of chat and banter with the staff. You need to know them and know their background so that you can discuss their children growing up and their grandchildren by name and age. They love that bit of talk. These are not superstars, film actors or celebrities, they are ordinary people who are looking to enjoy themselves. There weren't many like Margot Fonteyn who was only too happy to chat and wanted to know a little more about you as a person. This marketplace we are in now, they love to be remembered and recognised and to be able to talk to the owner. And why not?

They love it when they receive a wedding anniversary card in their bedroom on their big day and a dozen red roses for the lady. It makes it memorable for them and they want to return. They like that we are family run, especially when my sons David and Neil junior and daughter Nicola were involved for a while. They are used to our staff, many who have been here for a while now, and it is all still very family oriented.

To get there and still maintain the due deference of staff to customer had to be forged the hard way. It had to be explained that when a customer walks through the door or into the restaurant or bar, you, as a member of staff, step back and allow them to pass ahead and not barge in front of them. It's all attention to detail: clean shoes, dark socks; clean shaven unless they were growing a beard, and even then, only with my permission. Another pet dislike, as far as I am concerned, is pierced ears and jewellery amongst the men, adornments through the noses, tongues and other visible places for the girls. I warn them at the initial interview that they cannot work for me if they cannot follow my rules. They can do what they like when they are off duty and away from the hotel, but I wouldn't employ anyone who had a permanent pin through their tongue.

Customer service is crucial, helping with a suitcase, wishing them happy birthday with a glass of prosecco at the dinner table, a little cake and the staff gathering round and singing "Happy Birthday". Old fashioned, yes, but still widely appreciated.

The staff training was very arduous for me over the years, having to go to what we wanted our business to be modelled on. I admit I have personalised it and rarely have to remind the girls to clear away empty glasses and wipe the glass ring marks off the tables. Small details, but all important. Wendy is the same, particularly when she does her two days a week housekeeping. She will spot the smallest things and make sure they are put right.

We ask our customers how they think we could improve our business and you would be surprised how keen they are to chip in, make suggestions and give us ideas. I was told by one lady how much she loved staying with us but felt that one thing missing was flowers. She was spot on, but I had to explain that it was something we could no longer afford in the current climate. The extra money on gas and electricity alone extinguished any idea of filling the £100 we had spent on flowers each week in the past. They quickly accepted the absence of the colourful bouquets when I added that it meant saving one of my staff their job.

Part of moving our business forward is listening to our customers and acting when it is deemed sensible and of benefit to everyone. If it is a genuine complaint you have to take it on the chin. It is the way we have progressed from two star to four star. It has taken years to take us that distance, from Third Division to Premier Division. We are number one on Trip Advisor and every entry is genuine because we have never asked, paid for, nor falsified submissions.

It is not just the customers we ask how we can improve; we also listen to the staff who are in the thick of things and can sometimes spot an improvement that is needed. All the time we can improve, we are going forward.

When we opened our new cocktail bar I wanted Miguel, our bar manager and mixologist to have some experience of how things are done in five star hotels. So off we went to London and sampled cocktails in the Savoy, Claridges, the Connaught and Browns hotels.

That is why we have a group of trusted friends who talk to us when they have eaten out and tell us what has been good or bad for them. I am also on the lookout when I go into London to dine or visit a five star hotel, observing everything around me to pick up ideas and tips to improve. I am not interested in what they might be doing wrong, only in what they are doing right and perhaps it is something I can take back to the Langham.

You can only control the controllable and while I can guide and instruct my employees, I have to put myself in the hands of fate with the clients who are a law unto themselves and can do things they would never dream of doing at home. When I was away on holiday, the staff discovered water pouring through the chandelier in the bar. A male guest had started to run water into the sink, put the plug in and then wandered into his bedroom to answer his mobile phone. It took him 20 minutes to wake up to the fact that water was pouring into the bedroom, but by then it was too late and right below the bedroom was my bar, with the water staining the ceiling and ruining a chandelier, one of a set of four. The ceiling needed attending to, I had to replace not one chandelier but all four because they no longer made the damaged fitting and it would have been ridiculous to have an odd chandelier. That one stupid mistake of leaving a tap running cost me a total of £800.

The culprit apologised profusely the next morning before departing, but it was another week before the ceiling had dried out sufficiently for us to repair the damage, covering the water stains and eventually giving the area three coats of paint. The staff member had to come in at 6.30am so that the bar could open as normal at 9am and as a thank you I gave him and extra £100.

As for the man who flooded the bar, it cost him nothing! I was told that I could claim it all back on insurance but that is not the case, as the minimum I can claim on my insurance is £500. So I am well out of pocket. He is a regular customer, so what could I do? Bill him? Not really, you just have to suck it up, and keep going.

Apart from the staff and the customers there is a third party – the coach drivers, and you never know what you are going to get there.

Do Not Disturb

Most of them are excellent, looking after their passengers, keeping an eye out on the elderly and infirm amongst them, while fitting in at the hotel where we provide them, through their company, with free board and breakfast. Occasionally there is a bad penny who can spoil it for everyone. I was busy working in the kitchen on breakfasts when I was called by reception who had a lady driver complaining that her room was not good enough, not cleaned properly and said that she had taken photographs and sent them to her boss. I got to hear about it and confronted her at breakfast and told her when she finished to come and see me. She could tell I wasn't in the mood for a friendly chat. I was upset. I don't mind someone complaining if there is a genuine cause, but I knew this was baseless and what is more she had sounded off to my receptionist in front of other customers and maligned my cleaning staff.

I have always worked well with the coach drivers, giving them a drink and generally looking after them, so that we could work together. But she had an attitude, a cocky little cow and I told her so. I was as polite as possible and asked her why she hadn't sought me out to talk about her complaints instead of mouthing off in public. She compared us unfavourably with another hotel where she had stayed opposite the pier, and I told her it would be best if she went back there, although not quite as politely as that.

While I was on a roll, I also told her that she was out of order charging her electric scooter in her room while she slept, not so much for the minimal costs to me, but because my insurance company had told me they were a genuine fire hazard when being charged overnight. The buggies for the disabled guests are kept downstairs and we charge them up for the guests so that they are ready for them in the morning. By 11pm they are unplugged to avoid the fire risk, even though it is less than the e-scooters, which are an actual, acknowledged hazard. I had to be tough with her and told her she should take it out of the bedroom immediately and stick it in the back of her coach.

She still persisted for some reason to criticise her room which was a single. Perhaps she expected a double with a sea view. I pointed out that the room was gratis, and she even disputed that, telling me that her employer, paid for it. She was on quicksand as I told her that she had a big mouth, didn't know what she was talking about and that her boss did not pay for her room, we did. I explained that I was the hotel owner, signed the contracts with proprietor, and that we provided the accommodation for the drivers out of the goodness of our hearts. I told her she needed to look in the mirror and grow up. That always bites, especially to a fifty year old. My dad had the perfect phrase, telling you to put your hand up your arse and pull yourself together.

The outcome was that I told the owners of the coach company what had happened and that I didn't want her near my hotel again. They fully backed me and joked I should have tossed her into the sea. I responded that I would if there was a next time and wouldn't call out the RNLI either. She checked out and took her scooter on the 600 metre run to pick up her coach, which had been parked down the road and I don't anticipate seeing her in my hotel again.

I do have the occasional contretemps with our coach drivers, such as the young lady driver who pulled up outside the hotel and having dropped off her passengers to check in, asked me where she could park. I explained that we had a contract with the army base down the road to leave the coaches there. I showed her a map, and explained it was first left and then straight down for 350 metres. The directions were quite explicit and clear on the map, showing it was no more than two minutes away. She was a bit flustered and asked me if I would mind going with her this first time just so that she could be sure where she was going.

It was only going to be a few minutes out of my day, so I jumped aboard outside the Langham and told her to take the first left 30 yards from our starting point. She sailed straight past as I tried to tell her to take the turn. She was flustered and full of apologies. I told her not to take the next left because, from experience, I knew it was too narrow to fit a coach and always clogged with parked cars.

Instead, I told her to go straight to the end of the road to the swimming pool, turn round the roundabout and come back towards the hotel. While I was telling her this, she took the next left as though I am not there and had not opened my mouth! I couldn't believe it. I asked her what she was doing, and she flapped worse than ever. Sure enough the road was packed with parked cars. Somehow, she managed to squeeze her bus through without wrecking any other vehicle before she turned left again into an even narrower street. I told her she was not going to make it and no sooner were the words out of my mouth than a horrible shrieking of metal on metal as she scraped along one of the parked cars.

In despair I said: "What have you done… wait a minute, that's my *** car!" She took the whole side out. I said: "You are having a giraffe (laugh)."

To make it worse she went back to her boss and blamed me for giving her the wrong directions. As if I would after directing coaches from my hotel almost every day. I had even shown her the map. What an expensive liar she was. It cost about £1500 for repairs, which I had to claim on my insurance. It was not cheap, and I made sure with the coach company that she was never given a coach to bring their clients to my hotel again.

It all adds to the stress, as did one of our guests who checked into her room and immediately set off for Beachy Head where she threw herself off the cliff. They found her a while later in the sea, near a secluded beach which is not much used in the winter. We knew about it in advance and had called the police when we found a suicide note she had left in her room.

It doesn't matter what your rating, there is nothing you can do in this sort of instance. It is appreciated that it is out of our remit and, like a natural death in the hotel, we can only comfort the bereaved and help them where we can.

As a hotelier you have to learn to cope with this sort of setback and it is all part of the way we developed from the two star to the four star rating, something that makes me and my family very proud. I am thrilled that we have achieved that, but there is no question of sitting on our laurels.

I was delighted when I had dinner with my daughter Nicola and her husband when they laid out a plan to start coming into the hotel a couple of times a week and helping, with a view to possibly taking it over when Wendy and I finally call it a day. She worked for me for three years, so has some background, but it was Wendy who pointed out that Neil Kirby was the Langham Hotel and that everyone wants to talk to the owner, whether it is for good or bad. She also pointed out that I had the hotel background that they don't have. It was terrific of Wendy to say that, but I also appreciated that Nicola wanted to help and free up some time for her parents. It is currently on ice.

It is not as if it is something you can leave to tick over, because there are constant adjustments and improvements needed to maintain standards and not all of them simple, cost free practices. The sea is beautiful and one of the main reasons I gambled on buying the hotel because of the wonderful view, but it is also a harsh task master with the salt air and the wind off the water battering the frontage which constantly needs painting and repairing, while inside the improvements we made when we first took over continue to demand our attention and our cash.

The first refurb of the larger rooms, the sea view junior suites, cost us £10,000 and the second £18,000, meaning we have spent an average of around £28,000 for these top rooms, all adding up to the near £3 million we have spent since moving in.

The bathing machine, a genuine piece of Victoriana, was a good public relations venture at £10,000, bought separately from the previous owners when we purchased the hotel, and it was last valued at £22,000, so a sound investment. I am told there are only three left in the world, one at Queen Victoria's Osborne House in the Isle of Wight, the one here in front of my hotel and one in a museum. There are many both in the UK and around the world, which have been left

Do Not Disturb

to rot in gardens or turned into garden sheds, but we proudly display the original that used to protect the dignity of the ladies as they shed their clothes on the water's edge before venturing into the sea.

Ours has its own little history, discovered in an allotment by the hotel's previous owners, with the wheels tucked underneath. They hark back to the 1820s when they were devised to protect the modesty of the girls and keep them away from the men who had their own bathing huts on a separate area of the beach. They refurbished it, had the paints matched up by Dulux from the scrapings that remained, and brought it back to its previous pomp. Queen Victoria's is a horrible shade of green, twice the size of mine and expensively furnished inside. That was turned into a chicken run when the Queen died, but happily it was restored to its former glory.

There is hope on the horizon as we continue to struggle out of the setbacks of the past few years, which have all taken their toll. Covid alone cost us £2.4 million in lost revenues, with the recent recession also hitting us hard, with fewer customers. As with any seaside resort anywhere in the world, what we really need is some good weather, plenty of sunshine and full trains coming into Eastbourne station. The promise of electricity and gas prices dropping further, an adjustment in food prices and the cost of fuel would all help. We are carefully working that into our budgets and to get our room rates right. We check them every day, just as you would stocks and shares.

We were developing our trade in our function rooms downstairs when Covid struck, and it has taken a while to reconsider what we should do about them as standing empty is a nightmare. The carpets alone deserve a little more footwear, as they were originally the handmade selection of Sultan of Brunei, as used in the Dorchester. A friend used to supply the carpets to the major hotels in Park Lane and he had to maintain a stock of spare carpet for repairs and replacements and when the hotels changed the pattern he was left with the old stock. So I have plush carpets made for the Grosvenor House in our corridors upstairs and the Dorchester carpets in the downstairs rooms and lounges. Both were one off designs and there is no sign of wear on either.

Neil Kirby

Our Bathing Machine built in the 1870s is now a local Landmark.

CHAPTER TWELVE
THE WORLD AT WAR

To run an hotel at a profit is not as easy as many people presume and it is something which has taxed my mind for several years as we slowly emerged from Brexit, recessions, a pandemic and a general downturn in ordinary folks spending power through massive price increases. If that wasn't enough, we then had the invasion of Ukraine by the Russians which had a global effect on the hotel business, including the United Kingdom. Then came the massacre in Israel when Hamas militants made an unprecedented attack with 1,200 killed and 250 hostages taken into Gaza, leading to an Israeli invasion as they tried to rescue the lost souls and destroy the terrorists.

Closer to home there was also the problem with the immigrants landing just down the coast from Eastbourne following their treacherous ride from the French coast in inflatable dinghies. You fight it or fail, and if you don't believe me just look around at the hotels that are shuttered and boarded up.

At the Strand Hotel next door to me, the owner opened his doors to some of the thousands of migrants who flooded in and made a nice profit and good luck to him. They have all gone now and he employed eight people to paint and decorate for several months, buying curtains and carpeting, and getting his hotel up to the standard where he can attract private customers and bring the coach parties back.

I had phone calls from the Home Office agency three times asking if I would be willing to take 140 refugees and each time I refused. It was tempting, the hotels who did take them in were paid £65 per person per day. I could have made a million pounds profit a year like my neighbour but my first thought was what would happen to my regular guests? What would happen to my staff?

What people don't think about is the staff who were made redundant when hotels were opened up to migrants. Their overheads were low, food was sent in from outside caterers so no restaurant or chefs required. The hotel next door to us kept on three chambermaids and two maintenance men, 40 members of staff lost their jobs. No wonder they made a million profit in a year! All around the country 342 hotels were filled with refugees, with 90% of their staff being made redundant.

It was only after the visitors had scattered to all parts of the country that we appreciated the effect it had on the town and its businesses. I did not realise at the time that the government provided free bicycles for the migrants, and these were all parked and chained to the frontage of the hotels they were using and then left when they departed. A mess that didn't look good to the paying visitors.

I trust that the other hotels will bring them up to scratch and start letting rooms out to holidaymakers which will be good for everybody in Eastbourne, as people come into the town prepared to spend money on food and entertainment as well as their lodgings. For that to happen the place has to smarten up and look the part, a place where people want to come to relax.

The boards are coming down from the windows, the bikes have been removed, the decorators are painting the outsides and doing up the interiors to attract the tourists from home and abroad. It will be good and much needed for our town and its deflated economy.

It has forced me to think out of the box and putting on events has undoubtedly helped to keep us afloat. I have reached out and have attracted the local community and not just hotel residents. The secret has been to put on attractive lunches and dinners, but at affordable prices. We have an average of 98 people attending a typical lunch club, all non-residents and all paying just £40 per head for their meal, a free glass of prosecco on arrival plus a free glass of wine with the meal. Simple maths shows that's just short of £4,000. By the time the food is purchased for a three course meal, the chefs and the waiting staff

Do Not Disturb

paid, it is hardly a surprise that the £4,000 is whittled down to a total profit of around £350, with the remainder swallowed up by the cost of general hotel wages, electricity and gas.

It would be a different matter if all of the diners were also staying for the night at the hotel, for that is where our real profit lies, bedrooms and alcoholic beverages, particularly wine. Bedrooms are the biggest single profit earner in the hospitality industry, whatever the price and whatever the hotel, from £100 a night to £1,000 plus, depending on the hotel's star rating and location. Here at the Langham Hotel, of every £100 we take in bedroom charges it equates to £70 profit with the remainder going on wages of the chambermaids to make up the beds and the rooms, linen to be changed, breakfast included and all the wages from reception and throughout the hotel. The profitability is high but has still reduced in the difficult years. It used to be a solid 80 per cent, but since the downturn it has dropped by 10 per cent, a huge slice out of the profits and the pot used for refurbishments and improvements.

The second biggest profit maker is the booze. Let's be honest, everyone knows hotels and restaurants pay around £9 to £10 on average for a bottle for wine which is then resold for around £26-£27. It is a massive mark-up, but nowhere near the huge profit margins added for the big London hotels where a bottle of Louis Rodier Crystal champagne would cost the establishment £185 plus VAT to buy in which would then be sold to the punter for £500. At the other end of the scale, a bottle of average Spanish Rioja bought in for a tenner would sell at £55 or more - plus twelve and a half per cent service charge on top. I don't charge silly money, but I still make a fantastic profit on my wine and spirits. It is always pleasing to have someone in the best suite, ordering the best champagne, because I know I am going to make a good margin, balanced by the visitors for a themed lunch which, after all costs, may reward me with around £3.50 per head total profit.

The third big hotel money spinner has fallen off the cliff with the advent of the mobile telephone, wiping out the vast margins made by hotels for offering an in room telephone service.

The margins remain low on food and heavy on the bedrooms and beverage. We put the rooms up by about £10 or £12 per night on average every year to try and keep up with inflation. It left us trailing but more would have just kept customers away in these days since the recession hit everyone in the pocket.

We would turn over around £4 to 4.5 million a year, of which VAT wipes off 20 per cent. The biggest nominal of profit and loss account of an hotel is the wages. In the old days it used to be reckoned that the wage percentage would be between 30 per cent and 32 per cent of total sales. Now we are running at over 40 per cent. The latest rise in minimum wage means that someone over the age of 25 doing the washing up will be earning £12.83 per hour, putting them on around £25,000 a year. It's great for the person, usually a man, who does the washing up, but it is tough on us to suddenly appreciate that wages have gone so much. At Grosvenor House when I did the washing up, I was on £12 per week, but that bought an awful lot more than it does now! I keep coming back to it, that the electricity and gas has made it tough for any business and has probably been the biggest single factor in so many establishments going bust in my field. The prices are coming down gradually but when you take a contract for a year, you have to suffer when that happens and hope it continues on the same downwards trend when a new contract is signed.

It has hurt us badly along with everything else which increased in price during the recession, especially food. I know I keep whinging about it, but it has hurt our industry so badly. Profitability on our business during 2023 and 2024 will be very low compared with previous years and the overall value of the hotel has diminished as a result. All we can do is batten down the hatches, get in as much business as possible, improve the occupancy to increase the revenue, put the prices up, while keeping them affordable to the clientele, try to keep the wages under control and find ways to bring in more revenue to somewhere along the lines of 15 to 20 per cent, remembering to always give value to your customers. It is tough and it is going to remain tough for a while, I suspect.

At least when you are not making lots of profit you are paying less VAT and fewer taxes but that is scarcely a consolation. Get the sales up; keep costs under control best you can; more you can grow those sales by getting people through the door by giving consistency in service and quality and people will come back. We have proved that at the Langham without dropping our standards. The same cannot be said for everyone as I look around. My competition in Eastbourne have been struggling, some won't bother to open until April for the new season; they are struggling to find the staff and will continue to do so when they fail look after the staff they have.

Many people are leaving the industry because they are being mucked around on casual contracts instead of full time contracts. I understand that aspect. Casual contracts suit us as well, because you can say quite quickly that we can't give the hours when trade drops off, whereas a full time contract means you either have to make them redundant with heavy financial penalties or keep them on with full pay when there is not enough work. We are having to have both full time and casual staff, which is unfair on the team, but that is life I am afraid until the economics of the country change. It is no use to anyone if we go going broke, because that would mean everyone at the hotel would be out of work.

We are struggling, not just our hotel, but everyone in the hospitality industry. One of the biggest problems for all of us is finding staff to fill the vacancies, especially chefs and waiting staff, jobs where there are split duties, starting in the morning, taking a break and then coming back in the evening, pretty well everyone hates that system and would much rather do a straight shift.

A kitchen porter does 40 hours a week and earns £24,000 a year and good luck to him. They do a hard job. You would have thought that with the sort of money on offer along with the perks, there should be queues outside my door but many are leaving the industry and stacking shelves at Tesco and getting the same money with regular hours and no stress.

The agencies who the trade use to supply chefs are charging £45 an hour, to be split between them. We can only hope that those who want to stay in the industry, the chefs and waiters, will come to the Langham, because of our reputation, both in looking after the guests and those who work for us.

It has been very tough, and it has forced the industry to change from the plushest of hotels in the city down to the old traditional seaside hotel. Customers are very demanding these days, understandably so. They are paying lots of cash to stay in the five red star hotels and the countryside piles and they demand the best. Automatically we are compared and while we are not five star, we do offer a personal service and are not charging fortunes for the privilege, nor adding on expensive service charges.

The industry really has changed. Hotels in the UK are massively behind where they should be in service, the food, the accommodation and the attitude of the staff. A lot of the places I visit are very average. It needs better training and better management, to first and foremost look after the customer and when things go wrong to deal with it, so they come back for more. Customers like their complaints dealt with promptly and properly and not ignored. That's why so many are turning to privately owned hotels for their vacations and their weekends away rather than the big conglomerates who have no feelings and crap service.

We care about our customers, and we want them to return to us whereas there are now too many establishments who do not give a toss what their clients think of them, and they are not concerned if they reappear or not.

In a 200 bedroom hotel there is probably an average of 15 grievances a day and 300 beds 20 complaints. At the Grosvenor Hotel in Park Lane, it was between 25 and 30, the bigger you are the more grouses there will be and around 90 per cent will be genuine.

The recession also affects the value of the property which varies considerably according to the latest obstacle thrown across our path, but it usually averages out between three and a half and four million pounds on a good day.

The mortgage will be paid off completely by January 2028 and then it is all ours and a weight off our shoulders, depending on how the hotel industry has shaped up to its problems in the intervening years. I still have lots of things I want to do in the hotel in that time, keeping up the standards and the quality for our customers with work on a new kitchen for the bar; keeping the bedrooms rooms up to the highest levels and to do something positive with the rooms currently underused downstairs.

We benefited when they were well used as conference rooms before the problems, which was another line of income. The introduction of online meetings from home has ended that and has left the rooms empty and forlorn. It has nothing to do with the prices we charge, but I am down to a couple of enquiries a year, so those rooms are going to waste and costing money as they have to be maintained to a high standard. Companies who hired them before have cut back and they no longer have to pay for the conference rooms, the bedrooms, the food they eat and the wines and spirits they drink. They have gone the same way as the hotel telephones! But while we have lost out so have they. The camaraderie, the spirit and the loyalty cannot be replaced by a computer screen with dogs barking and babies crying in the background.

It is the same with weddings, or it would be if we still held them at the Langham. People aren't having big wedding receptions because they cannot afford it. We don't want them and won't bring them back, because they were always more trouble than they were worth. Bob Brown, a friend of mine in the entertainment industry and our regular toastmaster, has lost loads of weddings, where he would usually officiate at various venues, because they just aren't there anymore.

When we first arrived at the Langham Hotel, the coaches ruled the business at £25 per passenger per day. Now it is £70 per person per day and a different sort of clientele. When I bought the hotel in 2005, I inherited the coach business. It was 98 per cent of the trade and the coach companies paid £25 for dinner, bed and breakfast. That price has now trebled with a limited coach trade. It may sound a big increase, but cost of living in everything has increased in 20 years! Those bits of business still pay the mortgage.

To my huge satisfaction, the private trade has grown and grown, and I am proud that I am able to take on highly qualified staff at all levels, although the choice is such for hotel employees, that you can interview and employ someone one day and the next they will phone and tell you (if you are lucky) they have got a job somewhere else or they just won't bother to turn up at all.

One of my ambitions is to offer the perfect souffle on my menu where you open the top and pour the sauce in. Small things but important in the bigger picture. I thought I had found the answer when I interviewed and took on the ideal man, only for him to phone a few days later to tell me he had accepted another position that suited him better.

That remains an expensive ambition while, on the other hand, there is also a lot of ducking and diving needed to keep costs within reason. We have taken to going to Tesco to buy our house wine, purchasing a pallet of 240 bottles of a popular wine like Sauvignon Blanc because I can get it cheaper than from my regular supplier in town. Go online and see businesses going bust, with hotels and restaurants selling their wine stocks to the receiver and they in turn sell it online in pallets, often for around £5 per bottle, a huge saving and a big profit earner which can also benefit our customers. It saves us around half the normal price per bottle and we are not talking plonk, but a decent non-vintage wine. It is another way of keeping expenditure under control and to balance against the wages which hurt us so much.

The hotel trade is, by nature, seasonal. We made £77,000 profit in December 2023 and then in January 2024 it turned into a loss of

£71,000. The reasons are obvious as December is celebration time with the hotel and the lunches all fully booked, then in January trade drops off as people take a deep breath and pull in their belts a couple of notches. On the surface it all looks good as the hotel is bustling and busy and even the delivery men who bring our meat, fish, cheese etcetera, tell us that we are the busiest hotel in Eastbourne, comparing us to the other hotels where they deliver. They all think we are rich and lording it, but the truth of the matter is that although we have people coming through the doors and paying an extra ten pounds, the costs have rocketed by at least twice that amount. Businesses have been put between a rock and a hard place and it cannot always be passed on to the customer because they will simply stop coming if they believe they are being overcharged or if they can no longer afford a weekend away or a candlelit dinner.

We have managed to keep a balance on our lunches and other events and while we don't make huge profits, they keep the business ticking along, keep customers coming through the doors and help maintain our contacts and friendships with the local community, who enjoy a day out at affordable prices in company they know and like. That trade has not dropped off at all.

It was back in 2008 I started my first lunch club with a speaker in the restaurant and had 43 paying customers. A month later I held my second and the numbers doubled – exactly! Eighty six attended, and it has gradually built to three or four events a month, and each one is sold out in advance and always with a waiting list. We have an excellent list of speakers and entertainers, which we hunt down with the help of a local lady, a friend of ours Angela Hughes, who used to run her own events and has a bulging contacts book. My General Manager Simon Brown and I sit down with her eight or nine times a year and talk about who is good and who is available, usually booking our speakers six months in advance so that the event can be publicised and sold through brochures, posters and word of mouth.

Neil Kirby

Comedian Tom O' Connor, Neil, Dec and Con Cluskey of The Batchelors at Langham Hotel.

Do Not Disturb

We also stage Gourmet Lunch Clubs; a Sunday Jazz Lunch and our latest venture, Murder Mystery Lunches. I know they have been knocking around since Agatha Christie was a schoolgirl, but they are still popular. I did my first one on a quiet Sunday in November and sold out. A lot of the clients are in their seventies and eighties, some have lost their partners and they come to enjoy the company and get very good value for money at the same time.

Whatever the function we always offer a drink on arrival and then with the meal, non-alcoholic if preferred, and then it is up to them what they want to drink at their own cost. In return they have outstanding speakers or entertainers, and they all keep coming back. The community say to me all the time that we have got it right with the food, the hotel staff and the speakers and that, if anything, we are too cheap! That is okay, we don't squeeze them dry, make just a small profit and they come back and maybe have a drink in the bar or a sandwich on the terrace on another day; perhaps they will use us for a birthday lunch or dinner; an anniversary party or entertaining visiting family members. They keep the wheels greased and keep the hotel busy. There is little worse than an empty bar, restaurant or terrace. No one wants to sit on their own in a place with no customers and no atmosphere. These people keep coming back because they know we can do it properly either for small parties or big groups.

Then we come back to one of our greatest sales platforms, the family atmosphere with Wendy and I serving the tables, along with the General Manager Simon Brown and whoever else is available. They admire us being hands on and it serves as good public relations. The live Jazz lunches are popular with roast beef carved from the trolley, our Sussex only cheese board and the ever popular crepe suzettes. We buy local where we can and when we can't we still prefer to buy British.

It is not just speakers at our lunches, we also have live shows with singing and dancing from the thirties and forties with the D-Day Belles; regular music with popular acts like Duality Paula and Barney Pout; Cheryl Baker of Bucks Fizz; Carl Greenwood trio, Roy Hilton trio; Anita Harris and David Hamilton; not to mention the popular staff Pantomimes and an Elvis Presley Dinner show. Our Gourmet Lunch Club features food and drinks from around the world including South America, Spain, Asia, Germany and presenting an American Thanksgiving lunch in November. We are bringing in more chefs to help Mike in the kitchen to continue his improvements.

We already serve great afternoon teas, but we want to make them even better by bringing in a chef who specialises in that area. We also focus on those specific occasions like Valentines Day, New Year's Eve and Mothering Sunday. People expect this sort of function to be full, but they won't be if you don't do them properly and charge acceptable prices. We seem to be doing things the right way because we had so many bookings for Valentines Dinner & Dance that we had to organise a second date so that it ran over two days, both fully booked. We featured the popular musicians Duality and Wendy provided chocolates with red hearts in the bedrooms plus the old fashioned Love Hearts with their cheesy messages.

Christmas is increasingly popular in the hotel, and bookings start as soon as Boxing Day is over and by March we are already more than half full for the four day package and the rest guaranteed to quickly sell out before we are through the summer holidays. The repeat business here is great, but it is bloody hard work. I am still doing over a hundred hours a week and Christmas week both Wendy and I did 116 hours.

I love Eastbourne and love the position of my hotel with its wonderful view of the sea, but I remain worried about the opposition. Not because they are challenging my position, quite the opposite. So many have been let go and are down at heel. I hate it because it can only drive people away. I want holidaymakers to come to our resort because they love all of it, not just my hotel. The more hotels working to capacity the more I like it because it means Eastbourne is busy and bubbling, not solely for the Airshow, Magnificent Motors, the Real Ale weekend or the Rothesay International Tennis Week, throughout the summer and beyond. I am not talking about the Hydro or the Grand

Do Not Disturb

Hotels which are of a certain standard. When I take a walk along the seafront from the Langham Hotel past the busy and thriving bandstand towards Devonshire Park tennis courts, I count the number of hotels that look to be on their last legs. It is criminal. What are they waiting for? Permission to turn them into apartments? Amongst the worst are the self-styled Sheikh Abid Gulzar, two properties with ceilings caving in and trees growing out of the masonry. It all looks appalling and can't be doing his reputation any good when holidaymakers see him driving around in his gold plated Tesla.

There is also a lack of investment by the council, with the pavements in a dreadful state, dangerous for the old people trying to negotiate the promenade on sticks or in wheelchairs. I am sad to report that in my first twenty years here in Eastbourne I have seen it go downhill, both the council and private businesses have let things slide.

At the Langham Hotel we are in what is known as the poorer end of the town, which is why I purchased it for a good price, but even so, whether it is here or in the town itself, we need clean streets and fewer potholes. There was an opportunity to do something positive when the new fibre broadband people came in to lay down their cables but all they did was make it worse as they came back over and over again, digging up the same streets more than once. I am disappointed with the lack of investment and the lack of forward planning. It is a great pity because there is huge potential with the beautiful South Downs, the miles and miles of seashore, an array of classical Victorian architecture and a lovely new harbour, where I initially had a flat. The state of the town is undoubtedly affecting my enterprise and a lot of other people too.

I am fortunate that we not only have our regular visitors from out of town but a most loyal group of townspeople who use our facilities and enjoy and appreciate our efforts to entertain them. I often ask people where they are from when we have our chats, and I am amazed how they come from the length and breadth of the country, and also from places like London and Essex. The statistics are all there in the computer and available at the press of a button, but I get more satisfaction out of talking to people face to face. It is almost like being a guest relations manager, one of the many roles I held at the Grosvenor House. I love meeting and greeting, listening to what they have to say about the hotel and the town, even hearing their occasional complaints!

Neil and Jay Blades during his stay at the Langham.

The Red Arrows and the Air Show, along with the Rothesay International tennis week, are always great business for me and the rest of the town. We are always well booked in advance for the big occasions and summer bookings are usually around 80 per cent during

Do Not Disturb

the week and higher at weekends. Like everyone else we put our room rates up for those special weeks by around £50 per night for both events. There are no complaints with the tennis tournament a traditional event which brings back return customers year after year, while the Air Show must be one of the greatest free shows, four days of outstanding entertainment for the cost of getting here.

Neil Kirby

Langham Staff getting ready to serve our guests Christmas Eve 2023.

CHAPTER THIRTEEN

LIFE AT THE LANGHAM

MIKE TITHERINGTON
EXECUTIVE CHEF
DEPUTY GENERAL MANAGER
HEAD CHEF

I am the man with three hats. I am head chef, executive chef and deputy general manager - but only one salary! It depends on what type of mood the owners are in as to what they are going to call me. I enjoy the diversity never been one for titles either.

I suppose that sums up my career so far. I was born in Eastbourne in 1975 brought up in Hailsham Town Farm Estate; supposedly it was a tough area at the time.

I guess I am like Mr Kirby because I started down the road at the age of 14 when I had a paper round and also worked on a market stall selling fruit and veg at the Enterprise Centre on Saturdays and Sunday mornings, as well as selling to some of the hotels and restaurants in town during the holidays. I worked for a company called Golden Fresh (sometimes not all that fresh) based in the town centre. Part of my job was to run fruit and veg into premises as a delivery boy; one particular day I had to drop some strawberries into town to one of the Italian restaurants. I was told to do it as fast as I could, not to talk to anyone, not to stop, just run them into the restaurant, put them on a table and run back out.

I did as I was told and ran into the restaurant, put the strawberries on the bench and turned to run out again. At that moment the kitchen door shut behind me and the chef and the manager barred my way out, saying they wanted to examine the fruit before I left as the ones that were delivered earlier were bad. They went through twelve punnets of strawberries and ended up with just four of a decent quality. They were not happy at all and started swearing and shouting at me. I tried to explain I was just the delivery boy and they should take it up with the owners.

I went back to the van where my boss simply said with a shake of his head: "You got caught didn't you?" It was fairly obvious, as I had eight punnets of mouldy strawberries in my arms, and told him they wanted a meeting with him right then and there and that was that. End of the contract. I sympathised with them for being cheated, but not for taking it out on a teenaged delivery boy.

I was into my food and had already started cooking by the time I was 15. It was around about then that I decided to be a chef, but I was equally determined I wouldn't treat people the way the owners, the restaurant and the chef had treated me. At the time I was cooking with aunts and uncles. None of them were professionals, just enthusiasts. It wasn't until I met my wife Claire at the age of 17 that I was exposed to that side of cooking. Claire's father was a baker. It was the first meeting I had with anyone in the industry. That was back in 1992 and Claire and we have been together ever since.

We make a good pair and Claire has followed me round the country, sometimes working at the same establishment as me and if not at another local hotel or restaurant.

I went to Eastbourne College of Arts and Technology, where I did a two year course on food and beverage, which covered almost everything. I was one of the last to do the old City & Guilds course at the time, but it has changed to NVQ. It was far more intense than it is now but far from putting me off, it only encouraged me. While I was studying, I also worked at a restaurant in town called Oartons in Bolton Road, owned by Ray and his family. I worked there Friday nights, Saturday lunchtimes and Saturday nights, plus the odd evening in the week. Often, I would go straight from college to the restaurant and then home to bed before beginning the cycle again.

Do Not Disturb

I did everything from washing up, making sauces, cutting up vegetables and prepping meat and fish. It was my introduction to how kitchens worked. I was 18 going on 19 at the time, as I had stayed on at the school for an extra two years. When I was 16, I went for an interview at the RAF with the idea of completing chef training. At the time I was told the military forces had privatised their catering to outside companies and the standards for the in house chefs were not what they used to be. I had enough points to become an RAF policeman but decided I would do another two years at school and then see what the situation was in their catering department; I should have become a policeman (joking).

I never regretted that decision. I had four choices when I finished at school. I could have gone to Canada, with the help of the owner of Oartons, who had been an executive chef over there while some of my family were Canadian, so I had the points to go there. I had interviews at Ashdown Park Hotel, London and Spindlewoods, which I eventually took because it was more one on one with fewer chefs. Added to this the owner of the hotel was a Michelin inspector, who knew all the ins and outs of the industry. Someone else I could learn from.

It was a 24 bedroom hotel; two chefs in the kitchen plus me to make up the numbers. It was very hands on so I knew I would get to become skilled far quicker than if I were in a big hotel or restaurant with lots of chefs and just being a number. It was a great learning curve cooking for the likes of Spike Milligan, Roger Daltrey from the Who.

After a year and a half I moved back to Eastbourne to work at the Mirabelle, the top restaurant in the Grand Hotel and spent the next two-and-a-half years there. I enjoyed it because they were a good team of chefs at the time and it was all fine dining, and they were going for a third rosette and Michelin bibs. It was traditional service but modern. The chefs and the waiters knew exactly what they were serving and could answer all queries; here I also did competitions from Escoffier to trying to be in the British junior team.

I left when I was poached by the head chef from the Mirabelle who wanted to be closer to his wife's family in Liverpool and had returned to the northwest. He wanted me to go with him as a sous chef in charge of the Sherlock Holmes restaurant, which was part of the Victoria and Albert Hotel in Manchester. Here was my first experience of cooking in front of TV cameras as Granada studios was across the road and l was asked to do a programme for Sky about up and coming chefs.

Claire was with me wherever I went so she was doing hospitality work as well at the same time I was developing my CV.

I was only there for a year before someone else came knocking and I was asked to set up a pastry department in Blackpool. It was something I had been doing at the Mirabelle. One of the chefs from the Grand had heard I was in the area and had spoken to the executive chef at the De Vere Hotel which, at the time, was part of the same group as the Grand in Eastbourne. I was beginning to feel like a footballer being transferred from club to club or, in my case, hotel to hotel. I have been lucky. Throughout my career I have not had to apply for a job, but have been asked to go places. Word of mouth, luck, aptitude, all played their part.

That, however, was a short stay as I moved back to Eastbourne when my stepfather Harry became ill. I wanted to be closer to home and I worked at a private members club, Bexhill Beach Club. It had only just opened, and they were looking for someone to come in and get it off the ground. It was a challenge, and I was there for about a year when the owners sold out.

It could have left me out of work for the first time but Rob Green, the executive chef from the De Vere, phoned me shortly before the collapse and asked if I would go and work with him at Down Hall Country House and Hotel, complete with its two restaurants and banqueting hall and just a short step from London.

It was a big job and I just over two years there with Claire as housekeeper. I was head chef of both restaurants and banqueting. The executive chef left, and I did another three months working his job.

I did some agency work after that for a while until I made up my mind what direction I wanted to take, whether to go into the pub trade, the hotel trade or restaurants. It was something of a sabbatical, but I fell in love with a pub, The New Inn near Hook, and stayed there for a year and a half working for a delightful couple, Michael and Natalie.

My idea was to learn the trade and then maybe take my own pub. Sadly I discovered after 18 months or so I didn't like pubs! If you are in the wrong place, especially if you are tied to a brewery meeting all their prices and their criteria, it is hard. That is why so many hostelries are closing. If you are holding back on your money, as many people are, why would you spend it in an iffy pub with a poor selection of beer and maybe not such good food?

After a couple of years I went to work with Jose and Marcia Vicos at the Toby Cottage, situated in Ripley just outside of Guildford. I spent five years there and the only reason we left was because Jose was retiring. He offered to set Claire and I up in our own restaurant, which was tempting. We went to look at a restaurant in Alfriston near the Star Inn; a couple around Ripley and another called the Duck on the Pond, a Michelin starred restaurant, which we both liked. He was prepared to put in £300,000, part of his retirement nest egg, which I felt was a lot of pressure to put on us if it went belly up for any reason.

The strange turn of events happened when the wine supplier, who also rented us our flat in Guildford, also supplied the wines for Mr Kirby at South Lodge. Neil and Wendy knew that Claire and I were planning to get married in Eastbourne and suggested we made use of the Langham Hotel, which they had recently taken over. I wasn't keen at all. I knew the Langham when it was tired and run down. We were persuaded to go and have a look and speak to them, and the rest is history.

It took six months for him to persuade me and that tied into my stepfather again because he sadly passed away and we decided to stay in Eastbourne. I ended up prepping the food for my own wedding. We were still making the wedding cake on the morning of the ceremony. It was a bloody good cake, too. Three tiers, a chocolate fudge cake, with white chocolate and vodka icing and fresh berries going round it. Robert Jones, the chef who made it, was someone I had worked with in several different restaurants. He actually came to work with me at the Langham for some months before he moved back to Scotland because his wife was expecting.

There is a point in life when you want to settle down and start your own family. Claire and I bought a place in Hampden Park, a twenty minute run from home to the hotel. I like to run and still enjoy running with Neil. We did the Brighton marathon together and the Eastbourne half a couple of times. I beat him every time, but don't tell him I said so! There is, however, a bit of an age difference.

I am happy because it is a friendly, family run hotel and it is nice to be somewhere where you are not treated like a number. They appreciate you and that is why we have been here for so long, 17 years as I write these notes.

When I first arrived, we were doing coaches and little else. We had a bar menu which wasn't doing anything. I would come in at 10am, finished in an hour, come back in the evening, do the coaching group and I was out of the door by 7pm. The change is phenomenal. We still start at 10am, other than the early breakfast chefs, but we are now open 24/7, always busy with lunch clubs, afternoon teas, dinner, and lunch. Neil has let me be the driving force in the restaurant, often talking about it when we are out running together. If we do Eastbourne to Pevensey and back, it is around 13 miles, roughly a half marathon. We talk about the hotel, the restaurant and life in general, and we are back in the hotel before we know it. They are good to work for and they look after us and treat us like a family.

There is the occasional brush with the customers, as there always is with chefs. With so much cooking on television everyone has an

Do Not Disturb

opinion and sometimes their ideas do not correlate with ours. Their idea of a rare steak may not be what I was taught. In one instance I was told by an irate diner in the hotel that it was not what they had ordered. They wanted it rare. I told them it was rare as requested and asked how they normally had it served. Cooked on the outside and pink in the middle, was the reply. I explained that was medium rare to any cook. Every chef is an individual and has their own way and own interpretation but, medium rare and rare remain what they have always been. The one difference is when someone wants it so rare it is blue, but that is not a frequent request these days.

I am not a violent chef as depicted by so many who make it as TV chefs. The industry has changed for the better. When I was starting you would see chefs throwing their toys out of the pram, cursing and swearing, but that is not my style, well swearing I may occasionally do. I remember having to prepare 120 croquettes for a function and the chef squashed 70 of them because they were not all the same size and shape. We were talking millimetres. What's the point? We all blow a gasket at some time, the heat can get to you in the kitchen, but we should never get violent, maybe just a few Hail Marys under my breath. I've calmed down a lot. I've never seen Neil lose his temper with his staff, only with customers when they are being rude to the people who work for him. They are few and far between and they usually end up embarrassing themselves in front of their friends.

Sometimes the customer is wrong, and the boss sees that and will stand up for his staff if they are right. In my seventeen years at the hotel, I have personally seen him tell two customers to leave, and they deserved it in both cases even the one where they both got carted off by the police. I often joke with customers l would have got less time for murder as l have been here a long time seeing people come and go not just staff but regular customers. We are all getting older, but yet I'm still here. l still want to make this hotel and the food we serve the best around, while still holding a few hotel secrets to myself, like working out AA inspectors or dealing with environmental health inspectors, but with all the stress this industry can cause we do have a laugh, me and the boss, and the family we work with at the Langham Hotel.

Claire and I still work together as she is part time at the hotel now, acting as group reservations manager and anything else that may crop up. She has the experience having worked for Neil and Wendy full time on reception when we first joined them, but now she has her work cut out with our two girls Maisee and Aimee who were born within a year of each other.

Do Not Disturb

SIMON BROWN
GENERAL MANAGER

I was brought up around the Camberley area and went to Collingwood School for my secondary education. I did a couple of years at Farnborough College of Technology, nothing to do with hotels, but studying television, video production and graphic design, something which has always interested me and is now a hobby, nothing more than a sideline.

Between 1991 and 1995, I was introduced into the world of hotels when my sister Hannah took a job at the Frimley Hall Hotel. She was doing part time reception work and told me there was a vacancy for a porter. It was good grounding because I undertook all sorts of roles there, restaurant, bar, night porter, receptionist and even night management for two days a week. I did the lot, a steep learning curve but, as it transpired, a good grounding for the future and I felt very comfortable going into hotels later as they are all very similar in terms of working practices.

I took a few months out, backpacking and generally unwinding, before I went to Pennyhill Park in 1996. That was where I first met Neil. I went in as a porter for a year and I had moved to reception by the time he arrived. I had been doing various jobs including duty manager and front of house manager and he soon became something of a mentor. He breathed fresh air into the place and had all the departments working together. He was the first general manager I had come across who was genuinely hands on, with his office right there in the heart of it all whereas other GMs I had worked for were more aloof and distanced. He just had a different way about him, the way he interacted and talked to people.

He did a lot of good things at Pennyhill Park and when he left it felt a bit empty. He had left a vacuum behind him. The guy who took over was the accounts manager and the inspiration was no longer there as it became money led.

Neil is very driven. He can never sit down for long, always looking for the next thing and little has changed over the years.

He then went off to the Royal Horse Guards Hotel in London in 2000 and he told me he would think of me when he was making appointments. I told him that I had wanted to work in London, and he invited me to join him, something which excited me. I enjoyed being with him again, as guest relations and groups manager, all very operational with the day-to-day running of the hotel.

Neil left after a year or so when South Lodge came calling for him. I remained at the RHG for just short of four years before I joined him at South Lodge in 2004 as guest relations, head concierge and duty manager, but when he left there, I really did not expect to be working for him again. In fact I remained there for six years and three months.

It is strange how life works. My wife Louise is a hairdresser and was working with Toni & Guy, a popular and well-established group, working with Trevor Sorbie, a celebrity hairdresser who was as inspirational to her as Neil Kirby was to me. He had opened his new salon in Brighton and took Louise with him. That was our move to the south coast, something which appealed to me. I was bored with the social scene, and I thought would like the buzz of Brighton as I did with London.

It quickly twigged that Mr Kirby was down that way at Eastbourne and I decided to give him a call. He seemed delighted and he had a role for me as revenue manager for a year then operations manager, more of guest relations and the day to day running of things.

South Lodge had been good to me with a real good team, it had been a good fit. When my first son Arthur was born and I wanted a role which would free me up more in the evening to be more supportive to Louise, a position came up in the sales office which I did for about a year, but it was not a satisfying job. It was a completely different world. It was a real challenge but not where I wanted to be, stuck in the office all day when I quite like to be on the operations side, mingling with the guests and the rest of the staff.

Neil had already planted the seed a couple of years before I left South Lodge, but I was reluctant to leave such a beautiful hotel. South Lodge was five star in a stunning setting, and I knew that Neil was having to haul the Langham Hotel up from where it had been left by its previous owners. It took me back to the first hotel I worked in, Frimley Hall, no reservations, events or HR departments, it was a bit of a challenge.

Now I think those guys I left behind at the other hotels have it quite easy because they have other people to deal with things they might not fancy. I made the choice to come to Eastbourne and I have really enjoyed it and never regretted the move.

I started at the Langham Hotel in 2011 when Neil appointed me as his revenue manager, a job I did for two years before being promoted to hotel manager and then elevated to my current position in October 2017. I have probably been here a lot longer than I anticipated but I am enjoying it after all the challenges of Covid and the rest, and more recently helping to put in a completely new digital property management operating system to bring us right up to date.

Covid was a lot more difficult for Neil than it was for me. I came in once a week, touched base in the office and then went home. I was furloughed, so on a personal level I was at home with my two boys, Arthur, Charlie and Louise, this was before George came along.

I enjoy my independence at the Langham, which is why I am still around. I like the fact we are not governed by a big company; it is nice to have that free spirit about running the place. Mr Kirby is the ultimate. He governs the place to the way he wants it, but I am so used to working with him I know his expectations. I love to explore new ways and he encourages me. We can disagree but these days he does seem to listen whereas in the past he would usually have his way. He is now far more trusting and open to new ideas. Given his whole long career he has his vision and his vast experience but now he listens to new solutions that are coming forward, especially since Covid.

After Covid he was understandably intense and focused on getting the business back to where it had been. This was not as huge a problem as it might have been because everyone wanted to get back and just be busy again. Once we were all back on board, he then mellowed somewhat. I have to remind myself he lives on the premises and never gets away from it, except on occasional holidays. In contrast I am away for two days a week and I try and forget business, while he can't. I am mindful of that. He still likes to get involved and never wants people to think he is sitting round doing nothing, something he could never do. He can never totally switch off.

As for my future I am not sure I will remain in hotels forever. I am leaning more into digital marketing which I went back into during Covid, selling a few drawings and found digital art, which I took an interest in. I enjoyed helping to put in the new systems we recently installed at the hotel.

At the moment life is good and I am enjoying my work, but if Mr Kirby sold the place, I doubt whether I would remain for long.

Mostly it is good fun but, inevitably, in hotels there are always the tragedies and the traumas.

We had a sad experience on New Year's Eve when one of our guests died just before midnight; and another when one of our regular bowls guests collapsed with a heart attack. But perhaps the worst for me was at South Lodge at a wedding when the mother of the groom collapsed at the reception. There were two nurses present which was a blessing because she had turned blue and it reduced the weight of responsibility I was feeling in such an extraordinary and heartbreaking situation. She briefly heaved a huge breath but then passed away. How cruel is that? The couple will have to live with the trauma on what should have been the happiest of occasions for the remainder of their days.

Do Not Disturb

LUIS MIGUEL RUSCIO
BAR MANAGER

I admit I was a disaster when I first arrived at the Langham Hotel and the biggest surprise was that Mr Kirby did not get rid of me in my first few weeks at the hotel. I did not make one mistake, but three, and he would have been quite entitled to ask me to leave after any one of them.

Not the start I wanted in my new home in Eastbourne, where I arrived in 2018 principally to learn English. I had been told by a friend who knows these things, that it would be cheaper and more enjoyable for me to work in a hotel rather than spend my money going to college and being broke.

I was born in Caracas, Venezuela in 1998, to a family who originated in Rome. I lived in Italy with them from 2014 for a few years and after briefly returning home to South America in 2017, I made the big decision to travel to England on the advice of my sister's best friend, who even directed me straight to Eastbourne to find hotel work.

I lived by the sea at home, and he told me I would have the sea on my doorstep again. I had done a year studying economics but thought I would be better served learning English which would open up the world to me. I had a big choice, England to work, or a scholarship to any one of four choices: Barcelona, China, Italy or South America.

I didn't want to study full time, but rather push myself forward, learn a new, useful language and take a course in investments. I worked long hours and spent little apart from holidays with my girlfriend Elvira who I met in England but who now lives in Spain. I visit her when we have a break every two or three months and she comes to Eastbourne in between.

I was happy with my selections, as I like Eastbourne and I am able to invest my money sensibly for the future. I really like Mr Kirby, especially as he was so understanding when I made my mistakes.

On my first week in Eastbourne I had to look for a job and the first hotel I went to see was the closest to where I was living, the Langham Hotel. I had no experience of the industry, and my English was not good. As I walked through the door of the hotel the first person, I saw was this very smartly dressed man who turned out to be the owner. I explained I was looking for a job but that my English was not all that it should be yet. I left my CV with the man who turned out to be Mr Kirby and he told me he would call me if they needed anyone.

As soon as I walked out of the hotel, I received a call on my mobile from Ali, who was the restaurant manager, telling me to come back and I had a job.

That first year was terrible, a complete disaster. I am only still here because Mr Kirby has always defended me. I was hard working but if it wasn't for Mr Kirby I would have gone very quickly. I was all over the place.

My first big mess was when we used to do lodges and big groups, which often went on quite late into in the night. On one of these evenings, Mr Kirby, who likes to keep an eye on everything, decided he was going to bed and only to contact him if anything went wrong. The evening had finished, and I was moving the meat trolley when suddenly the large, heavy lid started to open and come towards me. My first reaction was to let the trolly go as I did not want to have my hand crushed and bones broken. The trolley careered away and went straight into the still room, just missing the very expensive stained glass windows, straight through the wall at the other end. This was 3am and I decided not to wake the boss, but to go to sleep and sort it out in the morning.

The next thing I knew was Mr Kirby's face looking down at me as I woke up asking me how on earth I had managed to smash his wall to pieces. Anywhere else and I would have been straight out of the door, but he said that it was going to cost him a lot of money and he would take it out of my wages each month. I thought that fair, but he never did take any money from me, just warned me not to do it again.

Do Not Disturb

Two weeks later I messed up again. I was a very heavy footed person and wore shoes with big soles and would thump about the place. Close to the door to the restaurant, we had a coffee station for the guests to help themselves. People used to pile their cups on the top of the machine and as I walked through to the restaurant, I heard all the cups, 30 or 40 of them, crashing to the ground and breaking, not leaving a single whole cup.

Mr Kirby asked me how on earth I had managed such destruction and I tried to explain I had just walked by, and they all crashed to the ground without me touching anything.

It got worse.

He begged me not to destroy anything else in his hotel but two months later exactly the same thing happened, only this time it was plates as well as cups stacked very high on a shelf and as I walked past, down they came again.

He must have seen something in me because he reprieved me again. I kept my job and there was no more disaster of my doing. We continued to get on well together and I would cycle with him while he was running. I would also run with him and if ever he wanted anything at all, I was only too happy to help after everything he had done for me.

He also took me for a nice day out in London with his son David to show me how the best five red star hotels operated, to eat the best food and to sample the cocktails ready for our new cocktail bar. Mr Kirby prefers cash to credit cards and, indeed, does not own credit cards, mobile phone or tattoos. He was very generous with his tips but when it came to paying the bills he used his wife's credit card and we had the best, even eating at Brown's Hotel with very small portions for a lot of money. We spent at least £1500 on the day out and when we returned Mrs Kirby had been watching the cash machine tick over. It was Mr Kirby showing me what he wanted for his hotel in Eastbourne by going to the likes of Browns, the Savoy and the Connaught.

Neil Kirby

I always tried hard not to disturb Mr Kirby when he went to his rooms, but sometimes the situation demanded it, such as the time when we all listened to a man and his wife having a drunken row in their room very late at night. Suddenly the lady involved walked down the stairs completely naked just as Mr Kirby came out of his room to see what all the row was about. Three of us, including Butch, who has worked for the boss for a long while, chased this naked woman and her husband all over the hotel. Finally we had to call the police and it was all inevitably down to too much alcohol.

Soon afterwards I was working with Mr Kirby in the restaurant while his wife was in reception covering for holidays. A big guy came up and wanted his key to his room, but Mrs Kirby was convinced he was not a guest at the hotel and refused. He claimed he had been in the hotel for three days but clearly he was drunk and not one of our guests and his biggest mistake was being rude to Mrs Kirby. He needed to be ejected and Mr Kirby called me to help and be a witness. Finally Mr Kirby was forced to intervene as the man ran at him in a bid to force his way into the hotel. It was a mistake; Mr Kirby may be slightly built and into his seventies, but he picked up the guy and threw him to the floor in on movement like the hero in The Equaliser. We watched open mouthed and very impressed and while the drunk realised, he had more than met his match, he still tried to gain entry around the back, forcing us to call the police.

The police arrived in force and backed up Mr Kirby, agreeing it was self-defence and revealing that the man was wanted for breaking his parole. They took the drunk, who was also had a drug problem, back to his home an hour away, never to be seen by us again. The police told Mr Kirby later that he was on bail for beating his girlfriend. A good thing he didn't know at the time as he might have been given another good hiding, as the boss doesn't tolerate hitting women.

The boss and his wife rarely get away for holidays, so when they go, we try and make sure we do not call them unnecessarily and solve the problems ourselves. Before he went away, he called in the plumber and spent £500 clearing out the gutters and the drains, leaving everything perfect. The very day he left the pipes were blocked. We had a big party in the hotel on the Friday night with lots of girls who threw sanitary towels down the toilet causing a huge blockage and on Saturday morning the water, and worse, came through the ceiling.

Every time Mr & Mrs Kirby go away or even just out for dinner something happens. Just a simple dinner locally saw the electrics tripping in the hotel kitchen, no matter what anyone did it kept happening until, finally, we gave in and called the boss to tell him we were in despair. It was only when he was on his way back that Simon discovered that the electricians had recently mistakenly connected the outside wiring to the kitchen circuit and the connection had burned out, tripping everything. It was all fixed by the time he returned.

Mr Kirby has very high standards for his hotel, and he was more than a little annoyed when an elderly male guest came down for breakfast and then dinner pungently and unmistakenly reeking of urine. We drew it to the attention of the boss who had a quiet word with the man's wife telling her it was not fair on the hotel or the other guests and that he must shower before joining other guests in the restaurant. It didn't happen and the couple even refused to take their meals in their room.

Eventually Mr Kirby ran out of patience after friends of his complained that the lift smelled of wee and told the old couple they must leave. The coach was due to depart the following day, but he had had enough and told me to find out the cost of a taxi to take them both back to their home in Leeds. We were quoted £750 but after ringing around I found one who offered to do it for £565 and the boss paid him out of his own pocket, cash in hand to get him away from the other guests. He certainly did a big favour to the coachload of people who would have had to suffer seven hours of that terrible smell.

The expense didn't end there as we discovered this incontinent gentleman had soaked a chair in our lounge, another in the bar as well as his seat on the coach. That was another £150 cost to the hotel to have the chairs deep cleaned.

CLAIRE TITHERINGTON
GROUP RESERVATIONS

I was born in Wolverhampton in 1977 but had moved to Eastbourne by the time I was six when my dad, who was a baker, moved his job to the south coast where we had family in the area. We lived in Hailsham, and I attended the Hailsham Community College. It had nothing to do with catering and the closest I came to the hospitality industry while I was studying was working at the famous ice cream parlour Fusciardis, opposite the Congress Theatre.

I studied information technology and while I work a lot with computers now, it is all a bit different, but it was all part of the process of education and growing up. This was while I was trying to decide what to do with myself and my life and I did my part time job for a couple of years for the money and enjoyed doing it.

By then I had already met Mike when I was 15. We have been together ever since, mostly travelling round England together with Mike working in restaurants and hotels. I was also picking up experience, working in the hospitality business in bars and hotels, until we finished up back in Eastbourne.

We came back for family business, but were persuaded by Mr Kirby to get married at the Langham Hotel he had recently taken over. We did and there we have stayed ever since.

Mr Kirby is quite a character and if a customer complains he will listen and do something about it straight away if he agrees - but if he doesn't agree, watch out. I have seen him chuck people out if they are being rude to his staff and especially his wife; I remember two girls being quite rude to him and he just told them to go. That was it. No arguments. He is very much a "Get out of my Pub" sort of man and they and a few others have left with their tails between their legs.

He is very much a Peggy Mitchell type of character out of

Do Not Disturb

Eastenders. Barbara Windsor ruled the Queen Vic in much the same way that Mr Kirby rules the Langham. I see him as the ringmaster in charge of the circus, cracking his whip and keeping everything and everyone under control.

We had some lost property left in the room by a young couple and the man telephoned to say that his mother would come in and collect the left items. The problem was it was a bag of sex toys, not the first nor the last we have found in vacated rooms, and as a result a very embarrassed middle aged lady arrived at the hotel to pick up this bag of sex aids. She clearly knew what she was collecting, and she even admitted her embarrassment. Why would you send your mum to pick them up and, indeed, why would she agree to do it?

Mr Kirby, being in the hotel all the time, has to field any moans, complaints or long stories. He is very good and very attentive but when he feels he has heard enough, and the conversation is going nowhere, he has a secret signal to the staff. He will tap the side of his nose, sneak a look to make sure we have taken note, and that the message is clear: Rescue Me. One of us on reception will tell him he has a phone call waiting or not to forget that he has an appointment in two minutes time. The escape route!

While I am giving away secrets, we girls at reception also have our own little game, harmless enough, just taking quick pictures of unfortunates who happen to drop off to sleep in the lounge after a heavy night in the bar. It is all very sweet, and they are swiftly deleted, the photos that is, not the guests!

Whatever the circumstances, Mr Kirby will always have the backs of his staff. Solid if you are in the right and a few quiet words afterwards if you are in the wrong. You know it is coming because he has a certain deep laugh and when you hear that you know he doesn't agree with you. When he does have to talk to you, he always starts with a positive and then finishes with the negative. You wait for it to come.

He is different from anyone else I have worked for. You look after him and you know he will look after you. That is all very reassuring. There is never a dull moment, and the end product is that the staff are like family, with Neil and Wendy at the head. They are complete opposites to each other, with Wendy being the quiet one but always aware of what is going on around her.

We have lots of customers who come back, and they eventually become part of the wider family, as do the coach parties, their passengers and some of the drivers, although it must be said not all of the drivers.

You know where the line is when you work at the Langham. One of the lines for me is money and I am always on the chase, whether it is for the themed lunches or groups of clients who come regularly. They know now when they pick up the phone and I am on the other end, that I am after their money. I like everything orderly and tidy. I am not always perfect, but I try and keep on top of it.

I also look after the groups and the coaches, juggling the bookings from January to December to ensure we do not have a crossover with two or three coaches arriving at the same time. I ensure the contracts are signed, with the various groups, especially the bowls groups. I help them organise their fixtures, rooming lists, eventually sending bills out and asking where our money is in the nicest possible way.

I do four days a week but during the school holidays I cut down to three to look after my two daughters Aimee and Maisee, who are both just going into their teens.

We have settled with the family and both Mike and I love working at the hotel. We have our families around us. It would have been no fun for us or the girls if we had continued to move around. As it is we are settled in the area, they are at good schools and have all the joys of living by the seaside and all that it offers. They are lucky to have the life they have; they can grow up on the beach with all that fresh sea air. It suits us all as a family.

OSCAR JIMINEZ
RECEPTION MANAGER

I was born in San Sebastián in the Basque Country in the north of Spain where it is nice and green, just like England, although maybe a little warmer. We moved when I was seven to Zaragoza, a big city in between Barcelona and Madrid, where I grew up with my family and the place I call home.

Since I was small, I enjoyed learning English, even attending private evening classes after school to progress. It proved to be very useful as, when I turned 18, I was offered a job in New York as an au pair for one year. It was too good an opportunity to turn down to gain experience and I was fortunate that they were also a very nice family. I had to look after a seven-year-old boy, taking him to and from school, maybe swimming or some other pastime, and then the weekends I was free to do as I wished and, as I had friends living in Manhattan, it all worked perfectly. It was a great experience, and we all remain friends. After I left, the family came to visit me in Spain, and they have invited me back to their home in America many times. I haven't managed it so far, but I will go. It will be a shock to see them after thirty years, especially the "little boy" who is now a big man.

When I returned to Spain, I was soon anxious to go abroad again to broaden my experience even further. I was recommended to an agency in England who placed you in work experience at various hotels. My first appointment was an hotel in Torquay and when I arrived at Heathrow airport, I was asking how to get to my destination but with my accent, which was part Spanish and part American, no one could understand me and without mobile phones or the internet in 1990, I was struggling. Eventually someone stepped in, and I explained I wanted to get from Heathrow to Torquay. My pronunciation was so dire, he thought I said Turkey and sent me off to another international terminal for a flight to Istanbul.

I eventually made it to my bus and quickly fell in love with Devon, making a lot of friends in the year I stayed there. I struggled with the English and the broad Devon accents at first, but by the time I returned to Spain after a year, I was getting the hang of it. English proved useful when I returned home because I worked at resorts in Mallorca and Ibiza where there were a great many English guests. From there I went to Andorra and stayed there for eight years.

Andorra is a sovereign principality with a population of just under 80,000, landlocked on the Iberian Peninsula in the Eastern Pyrenees, bordered by France to the North and Spain to the South. I continued working at my hotel experience, starting on reception at the beautiful Princessa Parc Mountain Resort and Spa, then quickly moving to reception manager and, within a few months, the assistant manager departed, and they offered me his place, which I held for two years in this five-star ski hotel.

It was while I worked there, I met my wife Katherine in 2009, an English girl who came with a friend for a ski holiday. We talked, got to know each other and when she went back to England we kept in contact and after a few months she returned to stay with me. She didn't speak any Spanish and when the opportunity arose for her to take a good job back home as a trained dietician later in 2009, we took it as an opening. The recession had begun to bite, and I decided it was a good time to make another move myself and I returned to England.

I said I was happy to go with her, providing we found a nice quiet place by the sea! Her offer was for Hastings, so that fitted the bill, and we found a place to live in Eastbourne. She then went to work in Tunbridge Wells and eventually in Eastbourne. This was 2010, a year I remember well as Spain won the World Cup in South Africa, beating the Netherlands 1-0 in extra time with a controversial goal from Andres Iniesta. It was a good year all round.

We are settled in Eastbourne in with a nice house and two children, Tomas who was born in 2014 and Harriet three years later. I miss Spain, but we go back a couple of times a year if we can. I live in the Old Town, and we like the Downs, the sea, being able to go for walks

Do Not Disturb

in the woods and to take the children to the beach. They went to Pashley Downs school by the Downs, a lovely small school, and then moved to Ocklynge School. The names alone conjure up all sorts of thoughts.

I had arrived in England with no job and thought it might take me a time to find one but in under two weeks I had a response from the Lions Group, who offered me a job straight away and I stayed with them for ten years and everything was fine until the pandemic struck in March 2020.

Just before that my wife and I decided to go away on our own without the children for the first time and have romantic second honeymoon in Granada, back home in Spain. We arrived on the Friday and then the next morning the President of Spain made a statement on television that everything was to close down and our plans to see the Alhambra Palace, the museums, the Moorish Palaces and eat tapas disappeared. After two nights in the hotel we were heading home unsure of what was happening in the worldwide pandemic.

My wife was very stressed worrying how we were going to get home and see the children with the lockdown in force at home as well. We made it back but no sooner had I arrived in Eastbourne the hotel was forced to close and I was made redundant, closing the entire business and paid off almost all of what they owed me.

Katherine was working at the hospital, and she carried on while I was at home looking after our children. I was with them for many months, worrying about my wife in her job and what was going to happen afterwards to all of us.

When things began to open up, I began to search for another job in May 2021. Having brought my CV up to date, one of the first places I sent my details to was Mr Kirby at the Langham Hotel. I felt good about it and, unusually, I followed up with an uninvited phone call, we chatted and I was invited for an interview. He showed me all around the hotel and then called me the same day and told me the job was mine.

I again began as a receptionist. I liked the place. It was well looked after, and I saw a big difference in the maintenance of the establishment compared with my previous place. It was owned by someone who cared. He was on top of the business every day and from the background where I came from, he was completely different to any other owner I had worked for. He lived on the premises and worked seven days a week from breakfast until dinner – and more when required. He and Mrs Kirby both worked all day, every day. I was amazed. That also reflected throughout the hotel, because the staff bought in and treated the guests the way the owners treated us. It is reflected in the way staff treat people and look after the place as if it were their own.

Customers are always complimenting the staff and 90 per cent of that is down to Mr Kirby for the way he treats his workers, and we see how he cares about the business, and we follow his lead. It is a very happy family. It is probably the busiest hotel in Eastbourne, but we come to work happy every day… well… most days!

I used to be able to walk into work from where we lived, but since our move to Old Town, I drive in. The girls aren't keen on the late shift, so I often work late and don't want to walk home at odd hours of the night, especially in the winter and the drive only takes ten minutes.

I am happy where I am and lucky my wife has a good job, meaning we are comfortable with a nice house and holidays back in north Spain, where much of the tourism is still Spanish, during the children's holidays.

It is always interesting and very early in my stay I was working the desk and night when a girl came in and asked if she could have a Double Mac Cheeseburger. I was taken aback, and she repeated her order, saying she had seen a big "M" outside and thought it was a McDonald's. I am still looking at our hotel for a big M, other than the last letter of our name. Maybe that letter stood out in the moonlight, but my guess is that she was perhaps a little worse for drink.

Do Not Disturb

One situation I remember well was when one of our regulars booked in her usual single room round the back. It was an early check in and when she came across the housekeeper in the corridor, she told them she couldn't open the door to her room and, of course, the girl let her into the room number she was given. She stayed there all day, and it was not until after she had dinner that she came to the desk and said she thought she might be in the wrong room. She certainly was. She was in a Junior Suite and had made herself comfortable, windows open, the bed had been slept in and all her clothes were hanging neatly in the wardrobe. I helped her pack and move to her proper designated accommodation.

More recently a gentleman from one of the coach parties was immediately marked down as a possible problem as he was off drinking continually. One night, when the girls went to turn down his bed, they found him asleep in the bathtub. They left him there to sleep it off and when the bus was due to leave, the coach driver, who was already mad at him, dropped him off with his suitcase some way from his home, prompting an angry call from his wife blaming us!

One lady fell out of bed and slept on the floor all night and then called us in the morning for help. She had been visited by her children the day before and they knew she had problems but didn't care much to help her or to let us know.

Sometimes we have guests who talk for England, they can't stop. Mr Kirby has his own way of handling it when he is at reception and at the receiving end, giving us a sign to tell him he has an urgent phone call, pretending to talk to someone at the other end, saying: "One nut on the wall is a walnut and one nut on the chest is a chestnut. OK." With the bemused guest wandering off, while we fall about laughing because we know the last, naughty line.

We have found a man, not a guest, fast asleep in the bar and often the night porters see guests sleepwalking, sometimes in the nude and sometimes in their nightclothes. Not a pretty sight. It is all part of the traffic of a busy hotel and we wouldn't have it any other way.

SUE SWEENEY
HEAD HOUSEKEEPER

My working career did not get off to the most auspicious of starts. After leaving school in Portsmouth I became a live in nanny for a couple of families, but I had to give it up in the second household when it was discovered the twin boys in my care both were diagnosed with leukaemia. It was a shattering experience for me and I can't imagine how desperate it was for the family.

I needed something different and cheerful, and I went for a temporary job at Butlins Holiday Camp in Bognor Regis, a resort I had stayed at and enjoyed as a child. I was only going to stay for a fortnight while I looked around for another job, but I finished up staying for six years!

I would have remained longer but in 1996 I received in a call from my ex-partner Lisa who told me she was suffering from cancer and asked if I would return to Eastbourne to be with her. How could you say no and I didn't but when I returned it transpired that it was a lie to get me to return.

It changed my life again, but I am grateful in one important way because I have remained in Eastbourne ever since.

Having gained experience in the Holiday Camp, I turned to hotel work as a natural follow up and started at the Cumberland Hotel and then moved a few yards away to the Cavendish Hotel, where I settled for a while until I was unexpectedly made redundant. It led to another complete change in my lifestyle as I went into parcel deliveries until the Cavendish suddenly asked me to return to sort out a problem.

I did that for them and was promptly made redundant once again. Not a nice thank you! I then turned to bar work in The Hart, a popular local bar, where I stayed for seven years before making the best move of my life so far when I joined the staff at the Langham Hotel. I sent

Do Not Disturb

my curriculum vitae to all the hotels in Eastbourne and the only one to answer and eventually offer me a job was the Langham Hotel. I started on 20 October, 2010.

I worked in the bar for a year and filling in as a housekeeper for a couple of days a week as well, until the regular housekeeper fell pregnant, and I have been doing the job ever since.

I love housekeeping, the challenge of it all. The guests are fantastic but when they leave their rooms you have to be prepared for anything, sometimes the worst! They have been known to wet the beds which then have to be sorted out and replaced. We begin the fight to have the guest pay towards the replacement, but sometimes it might be a little old lady, leaving us with little chance of recouping our losses.

I have also had more than one guest who poo everywhere, older people who can't get to the bathroom quickly enough.

Then there were a couple of guests who become wedged in the bath and had to be helped out. Not at the same time, you understand! There was one poor man who was stuck, and his wife had emptied all the water out, leaving him not only trapped but totally exposed. Why was it always the man? I would hand them a towel and asked them to cover their dignity. Hard to believe it happened twice. The second unfortunate got drunk, fell over and broke his collar bone. He was clearly well anesthetised because instead of calling for assistance, he decided to have a bath and then couldn't lever himself out.

Sex toys are regularly left behind in rooms and, strangely, the customer never phones up and asks for them to be sent on! I wonder why? On one occasion one lady left a whole bag full of sex toys. She was not one of the Senior Citizens and we could only assume that she was here for business, and we didn't see her again.

Some make you laugh, and others make you sob. One lady booked in for a weekend with us and on the Sunday left her room, went to Beachy Head and jumped off. We had to call the police because we found a suicide note in the room. They discovered the body three or four days later in the sea. Sadly this was not the only time this happened. It is more often than not the housekeeper who is at the sharp end of events like this. When I worked at the Cavendish, we had a lady come in from abroad, checked in, dropped a case in her room, took a taxi straight to Beachy Head and jumped. That must be the shortest stay ever!

Here in the hotel, I have had two deaths. One was an elderly gentleman who was with a group. They were all waiting for him in reception ready to leave and had to send someone up in case he had overslept. He had fallen out of bed and died with a massive heart attack. The other was on a New Year's Eve when a lady in her nineties collapsed and died on the dancefloor a few minutes before midnight. She was a sweetheart, and we know she died happy. I met her family and they all said how brilliant she was with the grandchildren. She died with a smile on her face, in the company of her friends and she wouldn't have known a thing as it was such a massive attack. Two people who were staying with us that night, worked in the hospital, and they confirmed she was dead by the time she hit the floor. The murmur they heard was coming from a pacemaker.

There was another lady when I first worked here who was staying in room 143 and when it was time for her to check out, she wouldn't go. When I politely told her it was time for her to pack her things and leave, she kicked off and swore and cursed at me. I asked our owner Neil Kirby to come and sort it out and she told him she was going to take him on as well. It was so unpleasant, we had to call the police and even that did not curb her as she then threatened to punch the policeman. They had to carry her out. She had just flipped completely.

Every year we have a do for retired military and those in the single rooms often take the wrong door, thinking they are heading for the loo, only to find themselves outside in the corridor, usually stark naked and with no key to get back in. We have had a few of them over the years. I have had to take them a dressing gown to cover their modesty before showing them back to their rooms. But they are a great, if ever diminishing, group who love our hotel and we love having them.

Do Not Disturb

I have worked with some bosses who have been a real pain the backside, but working for Neil and Wendy has been a joy, they are the best I have ever worked for. If you have a problem, you can always approach them, and they appreciate how hard my girls work for them. It can be a nightmare at times when rooms have been trashed or where the guest has been sick everywhere. They just get it on and get everything done without complaint. For those who claim it is an easy job, I would just suggest they try it for a week, any week, any time of the year.

Mr Kirby always says that housekeeping is the hardest job in the hotel. It is simple enough to go out with a plate in the restaurant to serve someone their dinner, but it is what happens after that dinner and a few drinks that defines our work. It can be back breaking. I have around eight girls working for me, but I have two main ones, both Portuguese. Angela has been here for 15 years and Philomena for two years. They are the best workers I have had here. Philomena used to work at Fusciardi's, the famous ice cream parlour in Eastbourne now under new ownership, from seven in the morning until seven at night and she does the same here, coming in at seven and leaving at six in the evening. If needs be we always stay later, a reflection of the respect for our "governors". It is like one big family.

I have even done restaurant work as well when we were undermanned. I always said that was one area I would stay away from. But one day they we were shorthanded for a coach party which I could manage as it was just a question of distributing the plates of food. Normally I would struggle, being dyslexic, to write down the orders which is why I shied away from doing it more often. Of course, it can be a problem, but I just get on with it, the old fashioned way. It is no use moping about saying, I can't do this and can't do that. Just do it.

I was at a loss during Covid when we were forced to shut down, so I bought myself a bike and did twenty-seven-and-a-half miles a day. I live in Old Town and would ride along seafront down to Pevensey, on to West Ham and then all the way back. The miles quickly mount up. I am a workaholic; I love work and had to find something to do, or I would have gone insane. A 16-hour shift is no problem, in fact I love it.

The Langham is generally busy which suits me as I enjoy being at work. Simon Brown is a fantastic manager, so laid back and not in your face like so many. There is a nice balance between him and Mr Kirby. I missed hotel work when I was away from it when the pandemic struck. I like cleaning and I like being able to see the end result of things. I am a bit OCD and I am always looking to put even minor things right.

Do Not Disturb

ALIONA BATES
RESTAURANT MANAGER

When I was first given a job at the Langham Hotel, I had never heard of Eastbourne, let alone knowing where it was. Worse. My English was almost non-existent! Almost twenty years later I am still at the Langham, married to hotel chef Aaron, with two young children.

I began as one of the girls waiting at the tables in the restaurant. I didn't have any English at all, making it quite tough to settle, serve the customers and keep my job.

I am not sure I would have survived had I arrived a year later as, in 2005, the hotel was taken over by Neil Kirby and he immediately began changing the staff, getting rid of those he did not think could maintain the standards he was setting.

The previous owners, who had the hotel for a hundred years, were lovely people, but different from Mr Kirby, a businessman, a hotelier and 100% knew what he was doing, while my previous boss was sweet, trying to help but didn't always know what he was doing, creating more chaos as he went along, while his mother lived in the flat in the hotel, a strict lady who everyone was scared of.

No one wanted to serve her, so it was left to me and for some reason we got along well right up until the time Mr and Mrs Kirby swept in and began the changes needed to upgrade the hotel.

It was a long way from my home in Lithuania, where I was born in 1982 in a little town called Gargzdai before moving to the slightly bigger seaside resort of Klaipeda, more the size of Brighton than Eastbourne, where I studied to be a teacher at the local university. On the second year of my studies, a friend, Ksenija, and I decided to go abroad, and we finished up at Ross-on-Wye, working on a farm, fruit picking, warehouse packing and that sort of thing. We did that for four months before returning to our studies. I liked it so much, however, I wanted to return and when I finished my studies after four years, with local job prospects not being good and Lithuania about to join the European Union, I was sent to Eastbourne through an agency to work at the hotel.

I hadn't a clue what the job entailed or whereabouts in England the hotel was located. It turned out to be waitressing in the restaurant rather than cleaning, as I had pretended that my English was a lot better than it was.

Before I left, we were given an interview over the phone by the agency and when they checked my command of English, I had Ksenija sitting next to me translating and whispering the answers. So it could be said that I took the job under false pretences!

It was tough at the beginning, not understanding the customers or even the menu but, with no choice, I had to learn the language and learn it quickly. It was swim or drown.

When Mr Kirby took over our first introduction was when I walked into him while carrying a tray. Not the best of starts.

The first thing he did when he took over was getting rid of staff, including the general manager and some of the staff from the kitchen and waiting staff. Wendy Bugg was kept on as the restaurant manager, and I survived the cull to work with her for the next two years as changes continued in all areas of the hotel with new staff arriving, improvements and new things added.

Wendy also went after a couple of years, and I was called in one evening and was told she the news of her departure. I burst into tears and wondered what was going to happen to me. A couple of weeks later I found out when Mr Kirby called me into his office and asked me if I wanted the job.

It was a bit of a shock for me as I suddenly found myself doing a lot more, including paperwork which was very different from talking to

Do Not Disturb

and serving the customers. There was a lot more to it, including training new staff, but I learned and adapted and quickly got used to it.

It can be tiring, and it can be stressful, but never boring. Every day is different and every day you are meeting new people, some good and some difficult but always interesting. Every day is a new page.

There are many strange requests and often strange behaviour, such as the day a gentleman came into my restaurant for lunch and while I was serving him, I noticed to my horror that he not only had no shoes or socks but also his toes and his toenails were black. I was gentle with him but left him in no doubt that he wouldn't be allowed back in the restaurant unless things changed.

Another man came in for breakfast, gave his room number and sat down and ordered. We realised something was wrong with the room number as, according to our lists, it was vacant. We checked it again with the reception and him and asked to see his room card to check that we had the correct number. Suddenly he began stuffing the remains of his breakfast into his mouth, leapt from the table and ran out.

Then there are the people who order room service from us and the customer opens the door naked or near naked for their breakfast and you have to drop off the tray as quickly as possible and hightail it back to the safety of the kitchen.

Sometimes you think you have seen everything and something else crops up, like the customer who complained to me that she did not like round toast and preferred it to be square. I offered to cut it and it was laughed off, but I am still convinced she was serious.

In this business there is not only a large turnaround of customers but also staff, but it is a happy environment and I keep in touch with a number of the staff who have come and gone. I have probably had at least five or six, possibly more, assistants during my time here but many do stay for a long time – like me!

I am fortunate in that I always understood where Mr Kirby was coming from, so we have maintained a good relationship. There have been moments, but we have been honest with each other, and I always knew what he wanted from me. If I did something wrong, I always let him know as quickly as possible. He appreciates honesty.

It can be stressful having your owner always on the spot, living on the premises, but we have never fallen out and I accept that it is his hotel, and he likes to be in full control.

I always warn new staff that it is very different from having a supervisor and Mr Kirby, as the owner, is always there and when you drop a glass or a plate, he will tell you how much it will cost to replace and not do it again! If you spill tea on the tablecloth, he will see and tell you it costs two pounds to wash.

But from the other side, he has kept the hotel going, kept improving it and never letting things drift. He will always be there reminding you to clean this, clear away that and to prioritise customers' needs. That is why the hotel keeps improving and brings back the customers time after time. He is always there when you need him.

After 20 years the hotel remains as special to me now as ever, more so as I met my husband Aaron at the Langham. He was working in the kitchen and although we were both in relationships for the first two years, we got together 11 years ago. He is also still at the hotel.

We tried to keep it quiet at first, but gossip goes round a hotel very quickly and soon everyone knew. We had our first child, Samuel, in 2018 and then a daughter, Ariana, in 2023. I was off on maternity leave for both, coming back early for Christmas for the first and then taking the full nine months maternity leave for my daughter, giving me only my second Christmas at home in 20 years.

Mr Kirby was in shock the second time after a five year gap. He called me in for a chat to tell me he was going to give me a pay increase and I felt so guilty I had to own up that I was pregnant again. I still got my pay rise!

Both Mr and Mrs Kirby have been very understanding and helpful although Mr Kirby cannot keep a secret. I asked him to say nothing about the first pregnancy, but he can't help himself and actually announced it at one of the ladies' lunches in front of 90 people!

They were all regular customers, so I didn't mind, and I am still here. Twenty years later and I am glad to be back, it is part of my life and honestly it doesn't feel like 20 years. I feel part of it. The inside joke is that when Mr Kirby bought the hotel, I was part of the furniture and so he can't get rid of me!

WENDY KIRBY
THE FINAL WORD

Before we bought the Langham, Neil was working as General Manager at South Lodge Hotel near Horsham, and I was working as an administrative assistant at a support centre for dyslexic children in Croydon. Our original plan was to buy a newly built flat in the Marina which we would use as a holiday home at weekends and whenever Neil could manage to get away from work for a few days. We had paid off our mortgage on our house in Sanderstead and, although I knew Neil had always been keen to buy a hotel, I pointed out that having taken on a new mortgage for the flat there was no way we could now afford to look at buying a hotel. I foolishly believed him when he said he wasn't planning to do that anymore. However, whenever we came down to Eastbourne for a weekend or short break we would walk along the seafront, and he was always interested to look at any hotels that he had seen up for sale in the Caterer magazine. I went along with this to keep him happy, secure in the knowledge we could never afford to buy one.

We initially looked at the Royal Parade (now part of the Strand Hotel) next door to the Langham but it was in quite a bad state so that was a non-starter but then the Langham came on the market. Although the décor was quite tired, Neil immediately saw the potential and, although I had my doubts, I was always going to support him to fulfil his dream of owning his own hotel. In a way I was excited at the thought of taking on a new project.

If I didn't know what was ahead in the immediate future when Neil put all of our money into the venture, I certainly did after the first three months, when he was working his notice at South Lodge Hotel and I was left in charge of the hotel, the staff and the paying customers. My years in an office in the Grosvenor House Hotel before we started a family was scarcely the training for such a mammoth task.

We were obviously not popular with the staff when Neil started sacking people who weren't up to the job and not to the standard he wanted. He would go off to South Lodge, leaving me to face the anger and distrust of those who remained. They were not nasty to me, but you could tell they were not happy, understandable because they didn't know if they were going to have a job when their new boss finally settled in.

I used to return to our house in Sanderstead a once a week because our two boys David and Neil were still living there, and I had to check that the house was still standing. I was so tired I couldn't drive the 50 miles back in one go. I had found myself dangerously nodding off while driving, so every trip I would pull over into a layby for an hour or so and sleep because I was so tired. Nothing was ever said, the police never came to see if it was a drunk or whatever, and I would just resume my journey after my nap!

During the first few weeks Neil was worrying about not having the business he had expected and fearing that we were going to go bust. I listened to him because he was the one with the hotel experience and I was convinced that we were going out of business and were going to lose everything. In those early days we were both in tears because we were thinking we were not going to be able to make it pay. It was nearly all coach business at the start, and we were not turning over the money we needed or expected.

He actually said to me one day soon after that first month, that he thought I should go back to live in Croydon because he couldn't do what he needed to do with me in the state I was in. That stopped me in my tracks and made me realise that I was not helping matters, only making them worse. I was dragging him down as well. Also, our daughter Nicola and her husband Jim and baby Katie came to join us so that helped me feel less isolated.

At around the same time the head housekeeper retired, and I thought that was a job I could do. Before coming here my job had been in education and didn't understand the hotel business at all, whereas Neil had a lifetime of experience. I went off to run the housekeeping department which was better because I understood what needed to be done. I felt useful at last and that made a big difference. It also made me realise what a tough job those girls do making beds and generally cleaning up other people's mess. Sometimes makes you wonder what some of our guests' homes are like if that's the way they live. As far as I can see housekeeping is the hardest job in the hotel and I have huge admiration for the girls who work so hard every day to keep the place clean and tidy.

It was a year or two before I really felt I was part of the management team, probably only when our daughter Nicola left. She had been doing all the accounts and office work and I had to take over and quickly understand what needed to be done; the bills to be paid, the VAT to be paid, the staff to be paid. It was only then I really got to grips with the business.

It has all been a learning experience but even after all this time I couldn't run the hotel on my own. I can do all the backroom work, but I can't handle the staff stuff. I have never managed people before whereas Neil has experience in that area, when he was back of house manager and when he progressed up the ladder to general manager. People I worked with before were friends, not people I would tell what to do or tell them off if they did it wrong. We were all mates together. That's what I missed, I wasn't friends with the people I worked with anymore because they felt that I was one of the bosses, and they couldn't speak to me.

It has changed a lot; we are much more friendly now. The staff have, in the main, been here for a long while and we feel we are all family. I really admire the way Neil is able to handle troublesome staff firmly but professionally. They usually get the message that they aren't up to his standard and decide to leave before they're fired! We have also made lots of friends with guests who have come back again and again.

I don't mind living on the job, I am quite comfortable at the hotel. When we first bought the Langham, we used to go back to the flat at the Marina every night, arriving at 11pm, had dinner, went to bed and

Do Not Disturb

were back up by 6am to be in the hotel for me to start my duties as housekeeper an hour later. This was every day, no days off, and is probably why I was constantly tired!

Now I don't have far to go to work and the only downside is that now and again you think you have finished work, settle down for an evening together in front of television and there is a knock on the door because something has happened, the lift broken down or a guest being taken ill.

I have grown into the life of being a hotelier. I can cope with most things that are going on. We all muck in, doing the washing up, serving the tables, preparing breakfast, housekeeping, make beds, even appearing in the pantomime we put on every year for the guests. I help at reception and do a bit of everything wherever and whenever necessary.

We have been very lucky with our staff. We now have a group who get on together and some, like Claire and Michael, have been here almost as long as we have. They only came here to organise their wedding! That wedding was the best thing that has happened to us because Claire is just fantastic on the reception desk and organising groups, and Mike is a great chef. The food is his identity and he has used all of his experience in various kitchens to make this such a well-known hotel for the quality of our food. Claire had never worked on reception before. She had done housekeeping and was working as a pastry chef at the same restaurant as Mike, but she just slotted in straight away.

It is not easy for some of our staff who have to come in early, go home and come back in later for the evening shift, but they are a great team, and guests regularly tell us what a wonderful staff we have, how friendly and helpful they are. I sometimes think to myself, well that is how they are supposed to be, but then I think of other hotels we have been to where that is not always the case.

One thing for sure it is never boring here. There are always things happening with the guests, good and bad, while the staff, in general, get on. Obviously, there are always one or two who don't hit it off, but mostly they work well together.

Hopefully one day we will be able to retire. That is what we are working towards now, once we have paid off the mortgage. There is no point thinking about selling the hotel in the near future because they are simply not reaching the right price at the moment. We have done our bit, and it is a shame there is no one we can hand it over to. But even if we did that the stress would remain because Neil and I are the owners, and it would be hard to step away if you can see things that need doing with someone else in charge.

There are memories good and bad, happy and sad, but nothing here ever stays still. I recall returning to the hotel one afternoon and seeing an ambulance outside and then Neil being carried down the stairs on a stretcher with one of our members of staff, a Sri Lankan, standing there crying as he watched the bearers go past. At a moment like that the very worst thoughts prevail but I quickly found out that while it was serious, it wasn't a near death experience. It transpired that Neil and our son-in-law Jim were working on the rebuilding of the reception area and Jim dislodged a piece of material which crashed down, ripping a big gash in Neil's arm, that needed serious stitching. It is another prop for Neil, and he happily shows his scar, although he wasn't too happy at the time.

It was a huge gamble but all in all it has worked. The hotel is still busy, and we are still together after fifty years of marriage and enjoying life.

Do Not Disturb

NEIL KIRBY
THE FINAL FINAL WORD

So here we are 57 years in the hotel business, starting as a washer up at Grosvenor House Park Lane in 1967.

I have seen and been part of so many great, wonderful times, sad times, guests, staff passing away. I learned how to handle deaths, not easy to do. It takes many years of dealing with guests at such sad times, tears, sitting them down, being with them, calling their loved ones to break the news. This gives you good grounding being hands on and learning about how to handle situations that happen in the hotel business but I still have nightmares about finding the body in Flat 4.

When I was a Duty Manager in all the hotels I worked in, I learned how to deal with all situations, trouble makers, drunks, guests who won't pay their bill, you name it, I have always been there to deal with the customer and staff issues. That's how I learned from the start of this business, it's the only way to learn. Don't hide from anything, that's one of my mottos.

Looking after our staff for me and Wendy is one of our top priorities. We understand that our staff also have families. They need their holidays when the children are out of school so we help them even in busy times, we are here to help our staff and we work with them.

I really enjoy training our staff, Wendy and I are hands on bosses and I wouldn't have it any other way. Customer service, look after our guests "They pay our wages", speak to our guests. All our staff are trained to say "Hello, how can I help?", etc. When things go wrong we don't run away, we get straight down to the problem and deal with guests face to face. Guests feel happy we have been honest and dealt with any issues.

It's been very tough the last three years with Covid and now the recession but we will get through it I'm sure. Costs have gone through the roof, heating, gas, food, beverage, wages, our profit dwindling, but we have to work as a team. Come up with new ideas, work together, listen to our guests in these tough times. They can bring new ideas, savings, it's easy to increase prices but I want to ensure they keep coming back to stay with us. I think over the years guests in many hotels have been ripped off, hotel rooms far too expensive, tips averaging 12.5% – a joke. We don't charge service charge, my feeling on this is simple – guests should give if they want but not be pressurised into doing so. The bill sometimes in luxury hotels for dinner for six people with wine could be £500 plus service charge at 12.5%, too much.

Will I ever retire they ask? You're 72 years old and Wendy 71. I'm not sure as I write this book, but maybe it is time to say goodbye so we can both travel, see more of our three children and seven grandchildren, our friends and my sister Sandra. I have been locked into hotels all my life so is it time to say goodbye?

> The Leonard Cheshire Foundation
> *Park House*
> SANDRINGHAM
>
> The Chairman and Management Committee
> request the pleasure of the company of
>
> *Mr. and Mrs. Neil Kirby*
>
> to the Official Opening of Park House
> A Country House Hotel for Disabled People by
> Her Majesty The Queen
> on Friday 31st July 1987 at 3.00pm
>
> R.S.V.P. by 30th June
> Mrs Scilla Landale, Westgate Farm
> Walsingham, NR22 6DY
>
> Please arrive by 2.30pm   This card will not admit

A date for Neil and Wendy with Her Majesty the Queen at the opening of Park House.

Do Not Disturb

> ℝ
>
> The Lord Chamberlain is
> commanded by His Majesty to invite
>
> Mr. and Mrs. Neil Kirby
>
> to a Garden Party to celebrate the Coronation
> at Buckingham Palace
> on Wednesday, 3rd May, 2023 from 4 to 6 p.m.
>
> This card does not admit

Invitation for Neil and Wendy to meet The King at Buckingham Palace in recognition of their charitable work.

Wendy and Neil receiving the Eastbourne Business Award for Hospitality, Tourism and Leisure 2017

Neil Kirby

CHAPTER FOURTEEN
COMPLIMENTS AND COMPLAINTS

TOP FIVE GUEST COMPLIMENTS AT THE LANGHAM

1   Friendly and helpful staff

2   Cleanliness of the hotel

3   Excellent quality of food

4   Fantastic views overlooking the sea

5   Value for money and no service charge

TOP FIVE GUEST COMPLAINTS AT THE LANGHAM

1   Size of Room

2   Size of Bed

3   No Air Conditioning

4   Steak Overcooked or Undercooked

5   Room too far from lift

TOP FIVE GUEST COMPLAINTS IN HOTELS WORLDWIDE

1   Noisy neighbours

No matter what type of hotel you're running, where it's being run, or how big it is, you will have to eventually deal with guests complaining about noisy neighbours. This is troublesome for a variety of reasons. Your guests are paying good money to stay at your hotel and getting some peace and quiet shouldn't be too much to ask. In fact, it's really the bare minimum of what's expected of your hotel's service. To ensure you deal with it correctly, make sure to politely ask their neighbour to please keep their volume down because it's bothering other guests. Keep in mind that the noisy neighbours are still guests at your hotel and should be treated with appropriate respect.

2   No hot water

You travel all day, finally get to your hotel and all you want to do is relax by taking a nice hot shower. You turn the water on and … it's freezing. This is a common issue that hotel guests have, and rightfully so. While it may initially be seen as a "first world problem", remember that your hotel's job is to provide an environment that mimics what they're used to. And that includes having hot water readily accessible. If the issue isn't able to be fixed, make sure to move them to a new room or consider calling in a plumber.

3   Small beds

The reality is that many people may have unrealistic expectations of what a queen-sized bed (or any bed for that matter) should actually look like. Take the time to calmly explain that the beds are the correct size.

4   Temperature of the room

No matter what you do to try and prepare, this issue will find a way to rear its ugly head no matter what. While one person may find the temperature to be perfectly suitable, another person may find that exact temperature too hot/cold. I wish there was a one fix solution for this, but there isn't. Best bet is to handle it by a case by case basis and revert back to the "I'm so sorry for the issue" response.

5   Customers not agreeing with hotel rules

If your hotel says there are no overnight visitors allowed, then that means there are no overnight visitors allowed. Don't let a guest feel like they can make you budge the issue or can complain their way around it. This goes for all of your rules. They exist for a reason, see to it that they're followed.

LANGHAM HOTEL'S MOST EXPENSIVE SUITE

£350.00 per night including full English breakfast

UK'S MOST EXPENSIVE HOTEL SUITE

The Penthouse Suite at Claridges £62,000 per night

Unveiling a new level of luxury, this sky-skimming addition to London's panorama spans the entire rooftop of Claridge's. Glass-wrapped and studded with skylights, The Penthouse—a four-bedroom suite—is flooded with views of changing skies across Mayfair from sunrise to sunset.

Written across The Penthouse is the creative language of Rémi Tessier, who perfected his craft in yacht design. Organic and pure, straight lines flow across the individual wings, both with their own identity – but together, forming an effortless sense of harmony. In each are rare and refined materials: ziricote, Lebanese cedar, green onyx fireplaces and the distinctive burl wood dining table that forms a statement-making centrepiece.

Wrapped in London's most iconic sights, the distinctive silhouettes of historical landmarks and modern monuments lie in every direction, and expansive Royal Parks are at your feet. Take in the 360° panorama from the central 'lake' created by sculptor Andrew Ewing, then step inside where every aspect of this ever-evolving space reflects the cityscape beyond.

At a Glance

4 Emperor beds

Sleeps up to 8 people

Average size: 1100 sq m / 11840 sq ft

Do Not Disturb

Views: 360 degree out to London's iconic skyline

Expansive four-bedroom suite designed by Rémi Tessier, with a 400 sq. m garden and private swimming pool

Claridge's Suite Standard Inclusions

Your Claridge's butler offering a 24-hour service

Return private transfer to any London airport with our fleet of electric and hybrid luxury vehicles, alternatively helicopter transfer can be arranged

For stays of five nights or more enjoy a complimentary massage for each adult and a traditional English afternoon tea for each staying guest, served in the Foyer and Reading Room, once per stay

Fully stocked private in-suite bar

Guaranteed reservations and preferred seating in all restaurants and bars

Pressing for five items on arrival

Seasonal welcome amenity & complimentary bottle of Laurent Perrier Grand Siècle served chilled in your suite on arrival

Private mini pastry masterclass for our VIC (Very Important Children) in Claridge's kitchens run by our expert pastry team

Monogrammed Claridge's bathrobes, embroidered with your initials and lovingly packed to be taken as a gift on departure (maximum of two robes per occupied room)

Complimentary daily 60-minute PT, yoga or Pilates session in your private gym.

Printed in Great Britain
by Amazon